EXPERIENCE TIMELINE

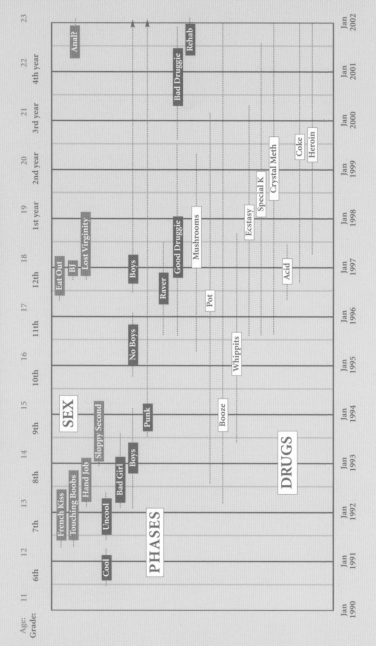

DEAR
DIARY

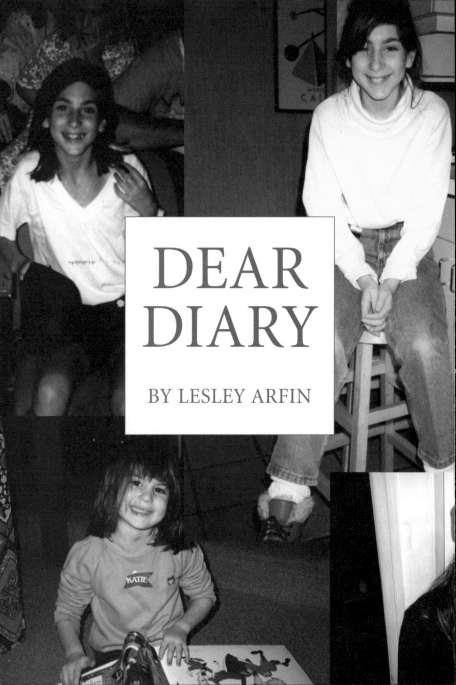

DEAR DIARY

BY LESLEY ARFIN

VICE

FIRST PUBLISHED IN THE UNITED STATES OF AMERICA IN 2007 BY:
VICE BOOKS
97 North 10th Street, Suite 202
Brooklyn, NY 11211
viceland.com

DISTRIBUTED BY
powerHouse Books
37 Main Street, Brooklyn, NY 11201
PHONE 212 604 9074 FAX 212 366 5247
powerHouseBooks.com

FIRST EDITION
2007 / 10 9 8 7 6 5 4 3 2 1

PRINTED AND BOUND IN CHINA

ISBN: 1-57687-383-8 / 978-1-57687-383-0
Library of Congress Control Number: 2007921801

THIS BOOK IS DEDICATED TO MY PARENTS,
PLEASE DON'T READ IT.

ACKNOWLEDGMENTS

Thank you Gavin McInnes, Jacob Hoye, Stacy Wakefield Forte, Vanessa Davis, and Chloë Sevigny.

Thank you Suroosh Alvi, Eddy Moretti, Shane Smith, Jesse Pearson, Liz Cowie, and everyone at VICE New York and MTV Books, Kathryn Frazier and everyone at Biz 3.

Thank you Scott Lenhardt, Meryl Smith, Emily McInnes, Cindy Greene, Carrie Imberman, Amy Kellner, Ben Cho, Mary MacCallister, Jen Brill, Marc Jacobs, Valentina Ackerman, Koozie Oas, Judi Rosen, Jeff Jensen, Ally Sklover, Julie Leventhal, Allison Farber, Bobby Eckstein, Gabe Rotter, Bill Strobeck, Scott Portnoy, Steve Cummings, Derrick Beckles, Tara Averill, Ramona Sidlo, Mike Strallow, Keeva Halferty, and everyone who participated in an interview or helped me stalk people.

Thank you James Palmer, Cris, Tony, and everyone who works at the Maritime Hotel.

Thank you Shelley Eisenberg, Bob Schnepps, all the Arfins, all the Dobbs, and my parents.

Finally I would like to thank my biggest supporter, my sister Kate. I'm sorry you're not in the book. The interview was kind of boring.

WHY I LOVE DEAR DIARY

BY CHLOË SEVIGNY

In 4th grade on the playground of Hindley Elementary School in Darien, Connecticut, I witnessed Katharine Whalen point to Sarah Brown and order her to tie her shoes. Sarah obliged, and that was the end of my pursuit of popularity. I would cry every day and beg my mother not to make me go to school. It was extremely painful. The girls were cruel, especially the rich ones. "You're poor, your daddy drives a Honda," they would taunt. It was during middle school that I found my niche, a tight circle of friends made up mostly of kids with single or divorced parents, children of alcoholics, new kids, bad boys, and general misfits. Luckily, I was blessed with an older brother who'd discovered skateboarding and hardcore, so I had a cool path to follow. By 8th

Left: "Peace in the Middle East," 1992; middle school; performing in
The Wizard of Oz; *homemade Slits jacket, 1994; New York City, 1994.*

grade I was in black-and-white striped stockings and combat boots, somewhat proud of my discontent. Growing up in such a small town, I really had no escape, and everyone knew everyone else's business.

During my freshman year of high school I carried over one close friend from middle school. She moved to Connecticut from Hermosa Beach, California, and was the worst influence in my life back then. The first time I shaved my legs was with her; she told me the boys wouldn't like me if I didn't shave them. The boys never liked me anyway, so I figured I had nothing to lose. It was her they were after. She had developed early and was known to put out, as were all the poor, big-breasted girls. I was her knobby-kneed sidekick with the too-big nose and braces and a laugh like a hyena. I was awkward as hell and unattractive. She was the first person I smoked cigarettes and pot with, got drunk with, snuck out of the house with, got arrested at the mall with, drove underage with, and all the other things us junior-high girls could get into. Sophomore year came around, and she got into dating thugs and hanging out in the projects. I got into new wave and punk. My brother was sent away to a school for delinquents, and I inherited the crowd he left behind. Freshman year was the only year that I can honestly say I enjoyed myself—though I complained about it every day. I fell in love with my brother's best friend, a senior. We had a crew. We never sat in the cafeteria; we were always in the smoking section on a picnic bench. That was our turf, and I was the only freshman allowed, thanks to my older brother. The seniors were the glue that kept us together, and when they graduated the next year, I found myself sitting alone in the cafeteria, listening to De La Soul or something on my Walkman. Eventually I found a hippie boyfriend who took me to pot rallies in Washington Square Park. New York City became my playground, and since I was only a train ride away, it was an easy escape. I made new friends from other towns and schools quickly, while the people from Darien thought of me as a junkie or a lesbian. They weren't mean to me, but they weren't nice, either.

When I first came across Lesley's column in *Vice* I was struck by a very familiar-sounding angst. Both of us were raised on 92.7 WDRE, both of us were bored outcasts from the suburbs of New York, and both of us narrowly escaped getting lost in the wrong crowd during our "bad girl" phase.

I loved "Dear Diary" because it took the essence of my insecure adolescence and wrote it down. It was funny, and a refreshing change from all the usual bullshit, especially in *Vice*, where it seemed like all the articles were written by obnoxious frat punks from Canada. "Dear Diary" was more *Sassy* than *Vice*, and it started a new genre—call it "grown-up teenager." Just because I wasn't a teen anymore it didn't mean I didn't tap into some of the same unwritten rules and fears that linger even today.

Of course, all of our stories and paths are different. While I did experiment with drugs, I didn't go to the same lengths that Lesley did, thanks in part to books like *Go Ask Alice* and films like *Christiane F.* I didn't have to try heroin to know it wasn't for me. Lesley's story is quite different.

What I love about "Dear Diary" is how strongly it res-

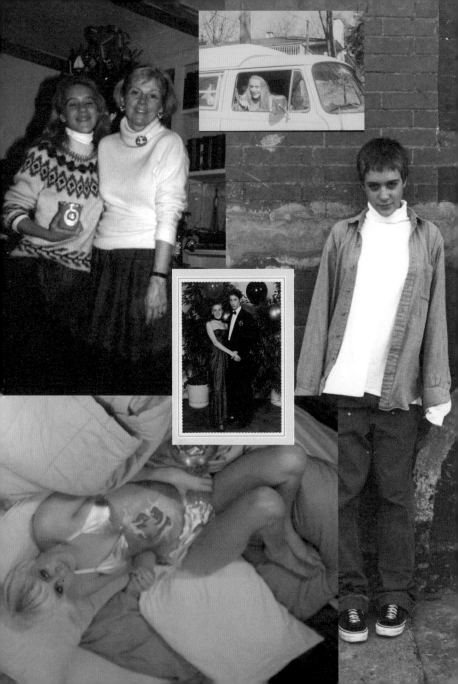

onates with all girls. We all went through a bitch phase that makes us cringe when we remember it. We tried being good, we tried being bad; we made other girls feel like shit before we knew what it felt like. I used to lie to my parents and tell them I was going to sleep over at a friend's when I was really going to Manhattan to dance all night and get high. When the car got broken into in the city I had to pretend it happened in the suburbs, which made no sense at all. It seems like the world is ending when you're 17 and in the middle of it, but looking back now I realize that's what adolescence is all about: making mistakes. And that's why I love "Dear Diary."

Left: Chloë and her mom; following the Dead, 1991; senior prom, 1993; first days of Washington Square Park; Rita Ackerman dolphin painting on stomach, 1994.

HERE'S HOW LIFE GOES FOR A TEENAGE GIRL

Wanna see your future? This book is my whole life, and give or take a few ridiculous circumstances, it's yours, too. Here's how it goes: You grow up in Long Island. First you're cool. Then you're not. Everyone hates you, and you get so insecure you start suppressing emotions by giving hand jobs and inhaling whippets.

Then come the bad-girl years. Sound familiar? If you just started smoking cigarettes and hanging out with boys who are rocking Guido fuzz, then you're probably too young for this book. See, when I was thirteen I was Virgina Slimmin' it and hanging out with people who celebrated Christmas instead of Hanukkah (I'm a Jew—this was kind of a big deal). I wasn't reading; I was too busy sending telepathic

Left: At Hampshire; in high school; kick line portrait from high school; summer camp 1991; road trip; dance recital; drunk 2000.

messages of love to Andy McDaris. Eventually, I got bored with thuggy boys and slutty girls, and Starter jackets were out and Stüssy hats with pot leaves were in. I listened to the Beastie Boys and Sonic Youth and heard the song "Institutionalized" by Suicidal Tendencies. I got punk. I immersed myself into a scene with other Long Island misfits who wore band T-shirts and chain wallets. This stage is kind of like your bad-girl stage, and from a parent's perspective it looks exactly the same. Only, Bad Girls do stuff like break into people's lockers and steal shit, whereas Punk Rock Girls do stuff like break into society and steal the right to put on an all-ages show and then donate the profits to Food Not Bombs.

Maybe you're thinking, like I did, that the problem with the punk-slash-hardcore scene is that it's just a microcosm of high school but with funnier hair. They don't wear clothes from Banana Republic, but they still all look the same. So fuck that. Become a raver! Do kids still rave? If so, break out the glow sticks (JK—those are for herbs). This was when I started doing drugs and got weird. It was awesome. I used to put blue eyeshadow on under my eyes so I looked like more of a crackhead. Throw some glitter on your bruises and work the room! Then I went to college and got even cooler and did more drugs. And more drugs.

This is maybe where our paths don't have to match. Because living out loud seemed like a great idea at the time, but when I graduated college I was a full-blown heroin addict with approximately zero self-control. I moved to New York City, hit what I thought was rock bottom, went to rehab, relapsed, hit rock bottom for real, went to rehab for real, heard Betty Ford do a speech, and saw God in a strawberry and now I'm better.

Right now you're either jazzed that our stories are so similar or you're AIM'ing your friends like, "WTF OMG ROTFL," and then going to get ready for your super sweet sixteen or whatever. It is, in a nutshell, one 12-year-old girl's trip from little kid to twentysomething. The graphs you see on the inside of the front and back covers are even smaller nutshells of this. One is a time line of all the people who helped mold my life in one way or another, and the other is a time line of all the "stuff" I did that made me who I am today. Maybe you're still in the I Hate Everything phase. I hope so, because this is when you can actually get away with it. It's fun to say, "My life so sucks right now," but it's the only one you got, and it doesn't suck. It's weird and scary and you get lost a lot but it doesn't suck. It's adolescence, and outside of zits, every bad part is kind of cool.

Inside you will find the long version of all this; however, there's an even longer version. It's called your own life. Try it sometime. You might like it. If you have any questions feel free to e-mail me at Lesley@viceland.com, but then, if you have any questions, you're not doing it right.

JUNIOR
HIGH

AGE 12–14

COOL & POPULAR

SEPTEMBER 1990 · 6TH GRADE-AGE 11

DEAR DIARY,

Tomorrow is the first day of 6th grade!! I am so nervous. I don't know what to wear but I feel like every year on the first day of school I blow it. I really don't want to get lost. That is the number-one thing I am afraid of. Number two is not having any friends in my lunch.

UPDATE · I had two really good friends in 5th grade (Amber Klinefeld and Donna D'Angelis), but I wanted to hang out with the cool kids in 6th grade so I pretended Amber and Donna didn't exist. Just like that.

The way you "break up" with friends on the first day of junior high is you don't sit with them at lunch, which is what I did. I walked right by them, and we never spoke again. It's mean, but it's a rite of passage every kid goes through at least once, like in *Freaks and Geeks* or *My So-Called Life.*

The next ten years went: popular and cool, then persona

non grata, then slut, then punk-rock chick, then raver, then heroin addict, then clean, then writing this book . . . But I'm getting ahead of myself. I was popular and cool for most of 6th grade, and I didn't write in my diary very much until April 18, 1991, when, overnight, I basically turned into Dawn Wiener from *Welcome to the Dollhouse.*

NOVEMBER 1990 · 6TH GRADE-AGE 11

DEAR DIARY,
When Mike asked me out it was a joke—thank G-d! I think I'm getting a math tutor. Halloween was awesome. Me, Sheryl, and Alli all wore skeleton earrings.

Alexis Frenched Ian. I've never really kept a straight diary like this. I hope when I die it's published. Like Anne Frank AND Laura Palmer! I just got Laura Palmer's diary and it is VERY dirty and VERY good. I know who killed her. Too scary to write. Well, it's B.O.B. but don't ask who he is. Today I went to the library and shopping and the best thing happened. I got my first bra!! Awesome. I [heart] you.
[heart] Lesley
PS—Beware Of Bob!!!

UPDATE • This was the beginning of 6th grade, and things were going very well. The only relevant person in this entry is Sheryl. She was the coolest girl in school, and after she built me up to the top of the in-crowd, she tore me back down.

MARCH 1991 • 6TH GRADE-AGE 12

DEAR DIARY,
. . . Every weekend I either sleep at Sheryl or Alli's and we have the best time. They never sleep over here but it's because I just hate my house so much. Alli's house is really big and both of them have really cool parents.

APRIL 1991 • 6TH GRADE-AGE 12

DEAR DIARY,
Hi! Me and Sheryl got in a fight but then we made up. Now Wendy is being really obnoxious and she's trying to trick me into saying bad things about

people but it won't work. I'll get back at her real good someday. I know I have a lot of friends but deep down I feel like I don't have any.

UPDATE • Ever notice happy kids don't write in their diaries very much? They don't have to. Life's too fun. Diaries are for when life isn't fun. They're for figuring what went wrong. On this day, things had just gone very, very, very wrong. I was no longer cool, and after this day I would never be cool again.

UNCOOL

★

MAY 1991 · 6TH GRADE-AGE 12

DEAR DIARY,

I know that everyone hates me because someone put a note in my locker saying the worst, meanest things I have ever heard anyone say to me. It was unsigned but I know it was from Sheryl. Gabe told me he saw my friends at 7th period writing the note. They made fun of my likeness of pigs. I think pigs are adorable! They also jammed my locker. Why? I do not know but why don't I say anything and fight back? Because I am stupid, ugly, obnoxious, and I hate myself. I wish I was never born! I wish that my family and me would be together and all the mean people would die. I am so fucking pissed I never want to go to school again. I don't believe in God anymore because he never helps me. Why are they like this? I need professional help. I hated my psychiatrist but now I don't really care. Why me?

PS The war has just ended in the world. It has just started in my life.

UPDATE · **Lesley: Why did I go to therapy in 6th grade?**
Mom: It was during that time—
No. It was before my friends were mean to me.
Are you sure? I think you might be wrong.
I'm not wrong. I wrote it down in my diary that I went to therapy in the winter. Friends were mean in the spring.
I was worried that you were depressed. You seemed to be manifesting symptoms of adolescent depression.
Oh come on. That's therapy talk. What was I doing that made me seem so monumentally depressed?
I think you were isolating, you were very moody. You were nasty, you were rude, and you were very withdrawn.
You do realize that all teenagers do that, right?
I can only tell you that I know now that all teenagers do that, but back then it seemed to be that your moods were more extreme, and I was worried about you. I was always a big believer in therapy, and I thought maybe there was something going on that you couldn't talk to me about.
Like what?
I don't know! You wouldn't talk to me! In the beginning of 6th grade you were in good spirits and then suddenly you were doing poorly in school. Do you remember when I sent you for testing to see if you had a learning disability? You were failing math and science. Things just started to fall apart for you. I remember talking to your guidance counselor and the special-ed teacher. They had you tested, and it turned out you had something called a visual perception problem.
Mom. Don't tell people I was in special ed.
They told me you couldn't see numbers lined up properly

and this was why you were having such a problem in math. They pulled you out of regular classes and put you in a special class for math, and everything turned around for you. You started to do way better. And you had that wonderful teacher . . .

Mr. Cascone. My boy.

Before we switched you, it had been affecting everything you did and you were really sad.

But then I got A's in math.

Yeah! Well the way they described it to me was that you didn't see numbers like normal people.

Well I think I see numbers like a normal person.

Well, maybe it corrected itself, Lesley. I also remember in elementary school when dad and me had to go to school and meet with all of your teachers and they blasted you apart. They said you were acting out in class and not working to capacity. Every one of your teachers had something negative to say about you. Then in 6th grade they wanted us to come to the school and do the same thing, what they called an "academic intervention," but I said no. I couldn't go through that again.

So I was always screwed up. It wasn't because girls were mean to me. I'd been having problems since 3rd grade.

It's not like you shared any of this with me.

Well, I didn't know how to communicate. I was 9.

I didn't know how to either, I guess. And then when you were in 6th grade, I was probably in therapy myself and she must have suggested that I send you to therapy, so I did. I was willing to try anything to make you feel happier.

MAY 1991 · 6TH GRADE-AGE 12

DEAR DIARY,

Sheryl and Wendy and everyone are being so so so so mean to me! I'm afraid to go to my locker in the morning and afraid to go to lunch. When I walk down the halls everyone either ignores me or says something really nasty. Why are they doing this to me? Nobody can help me. Not even you, so why do I even write to you? I HATE YOU!!!

UPDATE · Saying "Hi" in the hallways was a big deal in 6th grade, like the more people you had to say "Hi" to, the more popular you were. I remember out of the clear blue I walked down the halls saying "Hi" to all my regulars and they just ignored me. They would rub salt in my wounds by saying hi to everyone else. It doesn't seem that major now, but imagine having to suss out your friends on a "who will say hi to me in the hall" basis and then realizing that number is zero.

There was one girl who was nice to me back then, and the sad thing is I don't even remember her name. She was Chinese, and she invited me to her birthday party once. When I got to her house it smelled like ginseng and no one was there from school; it was just her family and me. I think I made myself forget her name. She represented the only member of the human race who actually thought I was cool at that time, and I think I hated her for that. Why did she have to like me when no one else could?

Everyone remembers the Sheryl Rosenthals and the

Wendy Webbs because they personify our insecurities. If we could only make our enemies stop hating us, we'd be perfect.

Nobody remembers the Lorraine Chans or whatever the fuck her name was. Lorraine represents giving up and accepting defeat. What a terrible thing to say. I mean, it's true, but poor Lorraine.

In September I wrote that my two biggest fears were 1) getting lost, and 2) not having any friends. After the Sheryl fight my two biggest fears were 1) walking down the hallway where my new enemies lurked around ever corner, and 2) *taking a number two* in the bathroom and having to read mean stuff about me all over the stalls.

Part of this book is digging up all the people from my past and finding out what went wrong. I found Sheryl in Queens, now 27, working two jobs, one at Kaplan (the place where kids prep for tests), and the other one has something to do with sports therapy.

Lesley: Why did you guys hate me all of a sudden?
Sheryl: I feel like Wendy wanted to be where you were, like with Alli and me.
She wanted to be BFF with you guys and bump me out?
Right.
Was it because of something I had done?
I can't really remember. I think rumors were started that weren't true. We were so mean. I'm always like, I'm definitely going to get a call one day where someone's on Maury Povich . . .
Can you make it Oprah?

I feel like Oprah wouldn't do a show like that, like a "You Were So Mean to Me and Look How Great I Am Now" show, like "I Hope You Weigh 500 Pounds."

Were you ever ousted?

Yes. In 8th grade we all had a falling out, and the tables got turned on me. I wasn't friendless, but I wasn't friends with Alli or Wendy anymore.

What happened?

I really have no idea. I'm assuming it was just your standard "Who can we be mean to next?" kind of thing. I also think that Wendy Webb orchestrated a lot of that from behind the scenes. I definitely think she played a huge part in how mean we were to you in 6th grade.

Do you remember who wrote that note? It was horrible. It said stuff like, "You think you have friends but everyone has always hated you because you're so ugly and disgusting. You smell like horse shit . . . " Do you really think I smelled bad?

I remember that note. Wendy was a big part of all that. Most of those things were from her. Alli was such a nice girl.

Yeah, but she was a follower.

I think I was probably afraid of not going along with everything . . . eventually it happened to me also in 8th grade. I remember going to someone's party in a basement and spending the rest of the night crying in the bedroom. It happens to all girls at least once.

And you can't remember what set it off?

All I remember is people were being different. They were acting cold. I was standing by myself and not really knowing why. And then having my mom pick me up, but I remember when you and I made up and how I almost felt worse just knowing what I had done and how mean we were.

We never made up, Sheryl. Come on.

Yes. We made up in art class. In 7th grade.

Well, at that point it was just easier to "make up." I didn't really care anymore. It made going to school everyday easier but I knew where my heart was and it wasn't there. So yeah, it was easier to sit across an art table from you guys, but at the end of the day I was just like, "Peace." It's interesting, though, because I feel like at that age, 11 and 12, it's sort of the first time in your life you start picking up on vibes. Fights don't become as concrete, the evidence isn't as tangible, but something is different and you know.

We were the popular, cooler kids. We were not only mean to each other but also mean to other people at school because we thought we were better than everyone.

I'm going to interview Wendy after this. You know she's going to say it was all you.

She was so mean! I feel like the idea of just bumping into her is scary. I've bumped into other people on the train and they were so nice. Even when I went to college in Florida I ran into people who suffered my wrath, but I feel like to run into her would be a little bit scary. She was the one who did all that to me.

I'm scared but then, I was scared to call you. Do you know what she's doing now?

I've heard stories here and there. One of my really good friends had a friend who went to college with her and was sort of in the same circle as Wendy and she told me how nobody really liked her that much, how she was a really big bitch. So maybe she's nicer now.

For a long time I felt victimized by you because you had done a lot of stuff to me. One of the reasons I wanted to contact you was to find out if I had done anything wrong or if it was just random.

Well, I definitely remember things, but to say you were guilty of doing something serious—absolutely not. It was probably stupid things like talking about people behind their back or liking a boy someone else liked. That's the way it always is with girls. We're mean. Nobody who got victimized in middle school did anything to deserve it.

I've always secretly wanted revenge.

I feel like I had it coming when it happened to me. It changed me a lot. I think without that I would probably still be horrible and mean and care a lot about things that I can care less about now. I'm kind of grateful for it.

Talking about all this is bringing up a lot of feelings I have.

Do you feel sad?

Absolutely. Yes. I mean, it's definitely a hard thing to stand up and go against your friends, but I should have. We were really good friends, you and I.

MAY 1991 · 6TH GRADE-AGE 12

DEAR DIARY,

Everyone is still being so mean and I mean EVERYONE. My mom just made me daisy shorts and I love them but every night I still have nightmares. Yesterday Jon and Billy were being mean and like, pushing me and yelling at me while I was on my way to Technology. I didn't think the boys hated me but they are just as bad as the girls. I went to the bathroom and there was mean shit written about me. It said "BARFIN ARFIN" as well as other things that I dare not say!!! School is over in 3 weeks. PS Wendy and Sarah were in the bathroom and they saw me in there crying and they started laughing and ran out. It really hurts!!

UPDATE · After interviewing Sheryl I realized I had to track down Wendy to find out why she ruined my life. She's also 27 and lives in Manhattan publishing books. She seems pretty nice now and has no recollection of being a condescending bitch, cunt, liar that made everyone feel like shit via weird headfuck, passive-aggressive evilness . . .

Lesley: When I interviewed Sheryl I asked her why she turned everyone against me in 6th grade, and she told me it was YOU.

Wendy: My retroactive memory of your history and mine is that I considered you somebody who I'd known forever, since early, early childhood, and then I remember we had crazy fighting and hatred in middle school. We kind of moved on from that and got over it but never really reconnected and eventually just drifted. I honestly have no recollection of a note or what happened. I wish I did. It's kind of strange that I wouldn't remember, which leads me to believe that maybe she's right?

It's interesting to me that Sheryl would say that. I don't even remember the three of you guys being best friends.

What I wonder about is that if Sheryl felt that way, why would she want to be best friends with me?

Well, I think she probably came to that conclusion later on in life. She also owned up to being a bit of a follower.

I felt like I sort of had that happen to me in 8th grade. Sarah, who I later became close with, did that to me.

You were ousted too?

Yes.

But the whole entire grade didn't go against you.

A lot of people did.

Actually, I'm acting shocked, but now that I look back I think I was happy you were ousted. I wanted revenge.

It was terrible.

I really trusted that you guys were my friends in 6th grade. We had sleepovers every weekend ...

I remember that more than anything else.

So you don't remember everyone being mean to me?

Now that you mention it, I remember it vaguely but only vaguely, honestly.

Do you think that you were a mean girl?

No.

JUNE 1991 · 6TH GRADE-AGE 12

DEAR DIARY,

School is over which is a good thing because I just about had enough. For some reason Staci Spitzer invited me to her party and for some stupid reason I went!!! Everyone was being mean and so I called my dad to come pick me up and he got out of the car and yelled at everyone. It was really the worst day of my life. I'm going to camp on Friday and when I get back to school next year I won't know who to hang out with or anything. I wish I went to boarding school. I didn't try out for cheerleading. I always thought I would but I just didn't care at all. I feel a little sad about that.

UPDATE · I remember that party. About five girls with thick eyebrows and clear braces cornered me. They told me in the nicest way to go home because everyone hated me and I wasn't wanted there. It was hard enough to muster up the courage to go at all, but I had this pride thing going on where I wanted to show my ex-friends that I couldn't be controlled, sort of like Bush trying to get rid of terrorism.

Can you imagine your dad going into a party and yelling at everyone for not being nice to you? I'm STILL mortified. That's as bad as having a skid mark or a period stain on your white pants. It's enough to ruin your junior-high career forever.

I guess it's better for them to care too much than too little, but at the time, sitting in that car, hearing the muffled sounds of my dad yelling at little kids outside was a fate worse than death. The real damage from that night was being betrayed by all my old "friends."

In 6th grade being best friends didn't mean that you were actually best friends with someone. It meant you had a place. You fit in somehow. It was social security for the most part, with a few good private jokes sandwiched in. I remember we had a list of 12 girls who were all "best friends," or "B.F.F.A.E.A.E." (Best Friends Forever And Ever And Ever). Some of the girls on that list I didn't even really know, but I knew it was cooler to be friends with a stranger than to have no friends at all.

BAD GIRL

✳

JULY 1991 · CAMP-AGE 12

DEAR DIARY,
I kissed Chad Hooper. We Frenched. It was very romantic because it was raining.

UPDATE · You can tell this entry is a big deal because it's short. The real heavy stuff is always brief. All my first-time sex and drugs stories are rarely more than a few sentences. Half of this is because I was scared of someone seeing it, and the other half is because I was kind of freaked out by the event myself and wasn't able to write about it.

This was all I wrote about my first kiss, but I remember a lot more. I told Chad I liked him, and 5 minutes later we were going out. "Going out" meant Frenching with second-base possibilities. This was at camp, the summer before I entered 7th grade. After we Frenched, which was in the pouring rain and very romantic, I immediately went into my bunk and brushed my teeth. Chad had been wearing some kind of cologne that was really, really bad. I feel like maybe his counselor gave it to him as a prank, but it smelled like old foreskin flowers. I wish I could smell it now. That way I'd have that sense-memory thing and I'd be back at summer camp having my first kiss as though not a day had gone by. I feel that way when I smell Drakkar Noir; suddenly I'm at the skating rink hanging with 7th grade boys who wear Starter jackets.

Anyway, I was turned off by the combination of the tangy perfume smell and his tongue worming around my mouth. I remember feeling slightly sick, slightly excited, and even a little bit sad. This was a turning point for me, and even though it was so long ago, I do remember feeling like I had abandoned a part of myself. I had crossed over the invisible line of adulthood and I couldn't go back. In camp all the girls were Frenching and some of them were even getting their boobs touched. I knew I wanted that too, but it wasn't because I desperately wanted to kiss Chad. It was more about fitting in. If you think about all the things you've done in your life and the real, honest-to-God truth as to why you did them, chances are you'll feel kinda sad too. I broke up with Chad about a week later and went out with Scott Shapiro.

Scott massaged my boobs during a rainy-day screening of *Hello Again!* starring Shelley Long. He sat behind me and touched my breasts under my sweatshirt, over my training bra. He literally rubbed them for the entire movie. About a week later I broke up with him, too. And then camp was over.

SEPTEMBER 1991 · 7TH GRADE-AGE 12

DEAR DIARY,
Everyone still hates me but I'm BFF with Marisa and Erin now. They go to South Woods but I know Marisa from Hebrew school. Erin was ranking

Sheryl out and then Sheryl called here and MY MOM ranked her out! So now I'm kinda scared to go to school. Marisa invited me to her beach party and I'll probably wear my crushed velvet bathing suit but with a T-shirt over it because I'm flat. My grandparents are coming. Oh shit I'm pissed!!!!!!!!

UPDATE • What is with my parents ranking out all my friends? NOT NORMAL! It was humiliating and it didn't make fitting in any easier. I'm not saying becoming a bad girl was their fault, but they didn't help matters.

When girls get ousted from the in-crowd, they either go the Lorraine Chan route and are loved by no one or they hook up with the bad girls. Marisa and Erin were the bad girls. They're both dead now. Erin died in 1998 in a drunk-driving accident, and Marisa died in 2006 from an overdose. Although I hadn't spoken to either of them for months before they died, they were a huge influence in my life right up until the end.

Marisa was the first one in 7th grade to develop. She got her period first, had big boobs, and her white-blond hair stayed white while everyone else's was turning a shade of mousy brown. She went out with older guys and wore classy mom perfumes like Red Door while the rest of us were still fucking around with Debbie Gibson perfumes like Electric Youth or, my personal favorite, Exclamat!on.

Erin, also hot, had these crazy blue green eyes that she knew were amazing because she would open her eyes real wide whenever we compared our physical features. She had pointy little tits and freckles all over her face and cleavage. Yes, she had cleavage. We were twelve. While everyone at Thompson middle school was arguing over which boy they liked and getting in fights over who started wearing choker necklaces first (it was me, BTW), Marisa and Erin were dry-humping 8th-grade boys in the bathroom and sneaking cigs behind the gym. They saved my life.

Speaking of cigarettes, I smoked my first one with Erin behind the diner one night (I was 12). When I was younger I used to put my mother's pack of Virginia Slims to my nose and breathe in deeply because I loved the smell so much, so I was pretty jazzed when Erin approached me with two flat-tened Virginia Slims still warm from her palm sweat. It did-n't taste or feel like my mother's pack had smelled (an exotic chocolate), and when she gave me another one, I put it in my pocket and saved it for later. Sadly I had forgotten that I had borrowed my sister's coat that night (it was a cool varsity-jacket-type thing), and when she found the stale Virginia Slim in the pocket a few days later, she told on me. I got in super big trouble, so much that I didn't smoke again until 11th grade when I tried ecstasy.

I didn't put in any interviews with my sister Katie because she kept saying, "Yeah, I guess," and "I don't know." She's 31 now, hot—in a WASP-y way (blond hair and blue eyes)— works in television production, has never had a problem with drugs, had OK grades, and was always pretty normal. She is basically living proof that none of this is my parent's fault because she was treated the same way I was and turned out just fine.

Dear Diary

DEAR DIARY,

It's been a long time since I've written (well, not that long). School started and me, Alli, and Michelle made up. YESSS! Sheryl and the boys still don't talk to me. Wendy didn't invite me to her bat mitzvah and I really wonder why. Maybe she really hates me more than I thought because we have known each other forever and even carpooled to Hebrew school.

DEAR DIARY,

Hi Diary! Sorry it's been a long time but soooo much has happened. I made up with everyone but Sheryl. The boys still don't talk to me except for a few. I went to Alexis's party and Brandon was being really mean. He kept making fun of my army-tag necklace! There's nothing else to write except for I LOVE DANCE!!!

PS I guess Mikki was right, everyone does hate Sheryl.

UPDATE · Mikki grew up around the block from me. We shared the same bus stop, as well as a hatred for the popular kids but a longing to be a part of them. We both kind of gave up that fight and joined friendship forces until jealousy overtook our bonds and we traveled in separate cliques. Mikki was tall and beautiful and had really frizzy hair that she later straightened. She was the first girl I knew to lose her virginity, and I think I kind of hated her for that. Once I even slapped her across the face and we both got sent down the nurse, Mrs. Bohner (her son's name was Richard AKA Dick), who was the meanest nurse ever to exist. We made up on the way down there because we were both scared of her.

NOVEMBER 1991 · 7TH GRADE-AGE 12

DEAR DIARY,
Halloween was amazing. I had the best time. There was no shit or Nair or anything. On *Beverly Hills 90210* Scott (David Silver's friend) died. He shot himself accidentally with a gun. Mikki and I were crying. My nose is still running. Today I went shopping and I bought shoe-boots and Bass Weejun penny loafers. I really hope I don't have to use Katie's old pocketbook. School just started. Whoopee. I'm not writing in you every day, only when something exciting happens. Nothing is happening right now.

UPDATE · Things were going pretty good here. This often happens when you get ousted. If you can bounce back and make a new gang of pals, the original gang loses. Sometimes the old gang will try to make peace with you and join your new gang. Ha. I didn't care about Sheryl and Wendy and what's-her-name anymore. I was over it. All I worried about now was getting my own pocketbook (purse) and not having to use my sister Katie's hand-me-downs.

When I was in middle school, if you did not own a brand-new Il Bisonte pocketbook on the very first day of school, then you were basically doomed to be a loser 4ever. BTW, "pocketbook" is the best word. I'm going to start a band called Pocketbook.

1991 kid's fashion was the best. Does anyone else remember shoe-boots? When you wore them under a pair of jeans it was like "Hey! Nice cowboy boots!" But when you lifted your jeans up it was all "Sike! Tricked you!" Unfortunately those went out of style quickly and Hotdoggers and Sambas came in. Hotdoggers are like Sergio Tacchinis for young, JAP-y Long Island girls. Sergio Tacchinis are what Mafia dudes from Jersey and old ladies from the Midwest wear—sweat suits that make that swishing noise. So a bunch of little girls got their fashion inspiration from Big Pussy and Dorothy Spornak but they flip the script by getting them in snazzy colors such as HOT PINK and NEON GREEN, and some even came with an exciting checkerboard pattern. The Hotdogger was what the '80s vomited up for the young miss of the '90s.

NOVEMBER 1991 · 7TH GRADE-AGE 12

DEAR DIARY,
Here's what's going on: Wendy, Sara, and Amy all like Alex Berkowitz. Wendy used me to get to Alex (Amy told me). Alex likes Sara. Everyone hates Sheryl and Jon Schwartz. I'm cool again!

UPDATE · Alex Berkowitz was my first boyfriend. We would occasionally kiss on the lips but never French or anything else. We went out in the 4th grade and then again in

5th, before I ever kept a diary. He had bright red hair and freckles, and his mom's name was Robin but everyone called her Sass (best nickname ever). I was over him by 1991, but all the girls started liking him, including my best *frienemy* Wendy Webb! So they'd use me to get to him, which made me furious.

His house was right on Woodbury Road; I still pass it all the time and think about him. He was so cute and kind of a bad ass. He also got me into Guns N' Roses. We remained on friendly terms throughout school, so when all the popular girls started liking him, they turned to me for guidance.

A friend gave me his IM and I chatted him up . . .

Lesley: Why didn't we make out? Were you shy?
Alex: I'm a puss. I was weak like that.
Why did we break up?
Probably because I heard that you liked some other kid, or someone else liked me. Some kind of 4th-grade baby-mama drama.
I think maybe I broke up with you because I was scared that eventually we would have to make out.
Hahahaha. That's great.
But I regretted it, especially when all these chicks started liking you in 7th grade, do you remember that?
Yeah, I actually did think quite highly of myself from grade school straight through 12.
When did you first have sex? Maybe I'm jealous because maybe I wish I had been the first.
Wow. I'm blushing.

Just kidding.

I had sex the first month of 9th grade; I was 14. Way too young.

Were you scared?

Totally! She made me do it without a condom!

Haaahahha!

Yeah. She basically raped me.

We should make out.

How do you know I'm not busted?

It's worth a shot.

Lesley has gone offline.

JANUARY 1992 · 7TH GRADE-AGE 12

DEAR DIARY,

I just read my old diary and I'm just going to concentrate on the future. Anyway sooo much has happened. I got to first with Nate behind the diner. Big deal, not! I'm sorry to say but my rep now is a "dirtbag" and there's really nothing I can do about it except NOT hang out with Corey Lyons. Oh yeah and I kinda beat up Wendy. I AM such a dirtbag! I hang out with hoodies and druggies! Who am I? Peaches 'n' cream or beer 'n' nicotine? I seriously HATE middle school. I have changed a lot and I am ashamed. I wonder if my sister has had sex yet? Nate wants me to give him a hand job but I won't because I'll feel like a used piece of shit. I just don't have the power to control myself from that stuff! I am being bad but having fun at the same time. My parents found a cig in my pocket!!! What is happening to me? I feel like a scumbag. Actually a JAP in scumbag's clothing. I don't know what to do. I'm scared to fight with Corey cuz he'll only get Hayley to kick my ass. I must go. I want to run away. Oh shit, somebody save me!!!

UPDATE • This entry is all about Wendy and getting revenge on the girl who ruins your life. It's something you think about the whole time you're a loser, but when you actually get there it's not as satisfying as it sounds.

Lesley: Do you remember when I tried to beat you up?
Wendy: I remember exactly where it was, outside the gym.
I guess it was revenge again for 6th grade. I'm starting to think that maybe I was the mean girl and you were the victim. Wouldn't that be a trip?
I remember you made me feel really bad and uncomfortable in chorus. It makes me feel terrible, though, to hear that I was responsible for what you went through in 6th grade.
I think the reason I tried to beat you up in 7th grade was because I was hurt that you didn't invite me to your bat mitzvah. I mean, we even carpooled to Hebrew school together! I was totally fucking embarrassed.
Actually, I remember something that happened before my bat mitzvah and that was it for me.
What was that?
I hate to bring it up because it's kind of sensitive even to this day. It was someone's bar mitzvah, I don't remember whose,

but your parents were there. Sheryl and me wanted to sit together and they had seated you in between us. We switched it around so that we could sit together, which is mean. You must have found out about it and gotten upset and told your parents.

Oh no . . .

Yes. Your father dragged me outside and threatened me. I was in 7th grade. I was hysterical and scared! This was like a grown person, a man . . . I was terrified.

No-o-o-o-o-o.

Yes.

So my dad started all this!? My dad ruined my life. He made you hate me and that's when I became a dirtbag?

I don't know, but I told my parents and then our dads had a thing. I think he called and said, "If you ever go near my kid again, you and I are going to have a really big problem." I guess I thought you knew about that, so then I just thought, "Well, Lesley and I can't be friends now no matter what . . . because I got into a fight with her dad." To me it was a big chasm in our friendship. I couldn't really get over it.

I don't blame you.

I kind of just didn't want to go near you after that. I was also scared because I had known your dad my whole life.

I feel sick.

I didn't want to bring it up and I didn't plan on bringing it up.

No it's good, I'm glad you did. This whole time I just thought you hated me for no reason and that's why when Sheryl told me that I thought it was true.

I had never been reprimanded like that by anyone, except for my own parents and it's just not as scary when it's your own parents.

Well, just for the record, I remember when I tried to beat you up. I felt very egged on by a lot of people. After I did it I felt so . . . I don't think I can remember ever feeling worse. I went home and prayed I could take it back because I saw you crying. I just remember clearly thinking that what I did was wrong. It was such a mean thing to do and I regretted it the minute after I did it and I never told you that. I'm so sorry.

You don't have to be sorry but . . . thank you.

DISCOVERING BOYS

✳

JANUARY 1992 · 7TH GRADE-AGE 12

DEAR DIARY,

I don't have any boyfriends and barely ever get to first in my life. It's probably because I make a brick wall jealous. I guess I care but there's nothing I can do about it. I just think that if anyone ever read this diary, I would feel like an outcast in this family. I would not be able to trust my own mother or sister. I wish I were 22. I would live in New York City and work as an actress. I would meet some guy and fall in love and live in his penthouse. Wild! I wish I were Marisa Goldberg. She is, like, perfect. Well diary, I am glad to have you to share my private feelings with.

UPDATE · Going to first is Frenching. Second base is touching boobs. Sloppy second is licking the boobs. Third is hand job and/or fingering. Sloppy third is anything oral. Home base is doing it. Why is a 12-year-old girl talking about this stuff? I was still three years away from my first period! They say girls try sex earlier and earlier every generation. Who's talking about bases now? 10-year-olds?

Most of my friends were only getting to third base (except for maybe Marisa), but that was three bases too far for me. I didn't want anyone to see how flat my chest was, let alone feel it for themselves. I remember a brief period of bra stuffing but that didn't last, only because my mom took one look at me and said, "Why are your boobs suddenly big?" I talked a big talk, but at the end of the day it was all about laying flat on my stomach and rubbing my vagina into my bed. That's how twelve-year-old girls masturbate BTW. I do remember that during this time I prayed every night for big tits. Dolly Parton tits. Can you imagine a 12-year-old girl with Dolly tits? Horrific. Anyway, my prayers were never answered. That was when I stopped believing in God.

MARCH 1992 • 7TH GRADE-AGE 13

DEAR DIARY,
Nate got a beeper. I really like him a lot. Erin is starting smoking again. She'll make me too. Why don't any of the guys I like ever like me? I want to kiss Nate more than anything and also give him a hand job. I want to run away or die but then I think of Mom, Papa, Katie, Dad, etc. I got a perm and I hate it more than anything. I hate my life!!!

UPDATE • Nate is an interesting character only because he was the hottest boy all throughout junior high and even high school. He was always sort of chubby and had a cool skater haircut, long in front, short in the back. Today he's still totally cute, but he lives with his mom and incessantly asks me if I can get him a job.

Girls fought over Nate all the time, and since he was such a sweet talker, he was able to spread his seed to just about every girl I hung out with. I had a weird thing about competition with guys. If anyone else liked the boy I liked, I pretty much just dropped out of the race. I still think that's a smart way to go. Basically, if a guy likes you he's going to go for you, so dropping out isn't going to lose him. On the contrary, it will make him like you more.

Nate: Oh just so you know, I went by Supreme the other day to see if they needed any help.

Lesley: And did they?

No, but I don't even have a résumé. I have to get a résumé, but I have to lie because I have no experience.

Well let me ask you a question about hand jobs and then we'll talk about regular jobs.

Shoot.

Did I ever give you a hand job?

Hells yes.

I thought so. Where was it?

I don't know. At your mom's house I think.

Was she home?

Yeah, she was home. We were in your bedroom. I also remember the last time you touched my cock.

When?

When you first moved to the city and you lived with that DJ guy. You got some shit (heroin) and asked me if I wanted to bang but I didn't want to. I slept in your bed and you stroked my cock. You didn't give me a hand job, you just touched it.

Who gave you your first hand job?

Leigh.

When and where?

On the bus. I guess 6th or 7th grade.

Who gave the best hand job?

Well, Tina was good, but she wouldn't bust out the lotion enough. Leigh was the best by far. She knew how to work the head.

Aren't you on parole for some stupid shit like DWI and not showing up for court or whatever?

I was on probation but I'm off now.

APRIL 1992 · 7TH GRADE-AGE 13

DEAR DIARY,

Last week at the fair Mikki and me tried a B with Corey. It didn't even work for me. I wanted it to so bad. Then dumb Mikki had to write me a note about it and my parents found the note!!! I didn't get in trouble but it was the worst thing ever.

UPDATE · This was my first experience smoking pot, or a "B" (bowl).

The Holy Name of Jesus Fair was a big deal in my town and within walking distance from my house, so Mikki and I walked down every night together. We had both wanted to try pot, and Corey was cool enough to hook us up. I heard that it didn't usually work the first time, but I was willing to take my chances. The McSheffrey twins warned me that if it did work, "Do not stay at the fair! You will bug out!" Immediately after I smoked the pot, Mikki and I just stared at each other, waiting for it to kick in, waiting to see if the other person was going to morph into a purple dinosaur. When we went back to the fair and realized that the first time wasn't the charm, I asked the McSheffrey twins if they knew where I could get acid. "Don't do acid at the fair! You will bug out!" They were identical twins; I was only able to tell them

apart by their colored contacts. They couldn't find me acid and so I gave up my quest to get high. Disappointed, but now determined. All the girls in my class read *Go Ask Alice* that year, the anonymous journal about a girl's descent into the dark world of drugs and addiction. After they played that LSD game "Button Button, Who's Got the Button?" I couldn't wait another minute to follow the white rabbit. The next day after the failed attempt, Mikki wrote me a note in school saying how we should try it again. I folded it up, threw it in my desk drawer, and thought nothing of it until I got home from school the following day and both my parents were sitting in my room. My dad was smiling and sort of trying not to laugh while my mom elbowed him, "Don't laugh Richard. This isn't funny." I don't remember if I knew what it was about, but when they calmly told me that pot was bad and not a good idea and never do it again, etc., my face turned beet red. I yes'ed them until they left my room, and when the fear ran out, I curiously wondered why I had been afraid at all. I was more shocked that they didn't think it was a big deal. I think that was the first day I realized I could get away with almost anything. Most of the time, I did.

Mikki's a teacher now. She's pregnant and living in Queens.

Lesley: Remember when we first smoked weed?
Mikki: Sort of. I do remember smoking weed out of my bedroom window all the time. I wound up in the hospital because of it.
What?
We were in town, walking somewhere, and we smoked weed.

I remember taking a cab home and—just so you know, talking about this is going to make me freak out—but I smoked weed and I got numb.

Holy shit I remember that. We thought it was laced.

I still think that. We slept at Carrie's house and I peed in my pants. Anyway, I was fine the next day and about a month later I smoked with my cousins and I got that numb feeling again. My entire body was numb but this time it was for, like, 4 days.

OH EM GEE!

I told my dad what happened and he took me to the hospital and they gave me some shot. I haven't smoked pot since. Any time I smell it or see people doing it I get flashbacks and I start feeling numb. I have to stop talking about this now.

APRIL 1992 · 7TH GRADE-AGE 13

DEAR DIARY,

I really like Andy McDaris. Like, I think I might be in love with him for real this time. I know I could get him but Jenny loves him and she's supposedly one of my BFFs. He called me a few minutes ago and we talked. He's different, shy, cool, funny, and sexy. When will I have a boyfriend that I like so much and he likes me back and no one is in the way? PLEASE PLEASE let someone like me!!!

PS CMH wants to beat up Brandon. So does Corey (that's my fault) but I remember all those times Brandon was mean to me in 6th grade and I'll never 4-get them. PPS Corey is going to my school next year!!!

UPDATE · What's with all the fucking gangs? What is this, Long Beach? I thought it was Long Island. This is a few years after "Straight Outta Compton" came out and everyone wanted to be a gangsta. CMH stood for Criminal Minded Hoods, a pretty tough gang for the suburbs (not). The level of crime at this point was about a 3 out of 10, no criminal records, just detention. DWS was our friends' crew. Down With Style wasn't tough, but they did do graffiti, and that's what they meant by being down with "style."

Corey was the worst kid in the district. He got kicked out of South Woods and had to go my school and got kicked out of there, too. We went out for about a week in 7th grade, but I dumped him because he told me I was flat chested. That and I think I was a little scared of him. He had no boundaries. We nick-named him "Boar" and used that term whenever someone was being an asshole, like "Quit Boaring out!" He cursed out teachers and threw chairs at people. He was hyperactive and annoying.

Corey got into smoking weed. He made some money selling it, got a nice car and a cute girlfriend to sit shotgun, and they just drove around all day smoking and selling and being extremely mellow.

After his family moved to Vegas, his mom shot and killed his dad. She got arrested but claimed it was self-defense and that he'd been abusing her for years.

Now, with the same girlfriend riding shotgun, Corey cleans chimneys in Long Island. No longer selling weed but still calm and collected. I told him about this book through a friend and got a myspace message that same day from his girlfriend saying, "Do not include Corey in your book."

MAY 1992 · 7TH GRADE-AGE 13

DEAR DIARY,

I am really over everyone these days. I am ready to go to high school or South Woods. I really wish I went to South Woods. I don't understand why I still haven't gotten my period yet. It's really ridiculous already. PLEASE ALREADY!

UPDATE · Getting your period as a young adult is embarrassing, period. Not getting your period when you're a young adult is even worse. Suddenly it became a hot topic in my family because I hadn't gotten it yet and although no one spoke about this to my face, I could sense a universal whisper throughout the household. Now everyone was waiting with baited breath for my period to come. I had to pretend like I didn't care; meanwhile I had to lie to the rest of the world that I had already gotten it. "Oh yeah, I totally hate cramps too. Cramps are the worst," I would declare at slumber parties. Or at the beach when the water was too cold and I was too chicken to go in the ocean, "Sorry guys. I am way too bloated. Does anyone have a Midol?" At first it was sort of fun pretending to have my period. It was easy. But after a few times I started to get a little sloppy with the lies, not realizing that it only came once a month, not remembering if I had already lied about it that month. I think in August 1992 I had my period four times.

Eventually I did get my period. My mom was worried and took me to the gyno to see what the problem was. The doctor told us it was pretty normal and that I was just a late bloomer. When I was 16 I finally got it, but by that point I had already had it for a few years because of my lies so I couldn't tell anyone. Like when I turned 21 and I had to pretend I was entering a bar for the first time. My advice to late bloomers: Lie.

FEBRUARY 1993 · 8TH GRADE-AGE 13

DEAR DIARY,

Last night a bunch of us went to Cooper's house and there were these guys there from Dix Hills that she knew from camp. I hooked up with one of them (Eric) but I doubt I'll ever see him again. I just wish somebody liked me. This kid was cute but he is in 10th grade and I know I just don't matter to him. So many people are OK with just hooking up except I feel like I always think about the person after, even if I don't know them or really like them.

UPDATE · This diary entry isn't really about thinking about boys too much or wishing someone would like me. It's about the first time I got fingered. That night I went to Carissa Cooper's house with a few other girlfriends, and she had some boys over who were friends with her older brother or something. I remember going into Cooper's bedroom with a boy named Eric who was not Asian but looked like he was. He turned the lights off and we both got on the bed. You know how when you get so nervous sometimes you stretch and yawn a bunch? I remember yawning nonstop and stretching like crazy. I was also shaking a little bit and would have had stinky pits if I was old enough to get them.

While we were kissing he started fumbling around with the zipper of his jeans. He then took my hand and placed it on his dick, curving my fingers around the shaft and moving my hand up and down and up and down like he was beating off but my hand got caught in there like an extraneous piece of machinery, a "wrench in the works," if you will. Boys do that when you're 13 because boys are assholes. While I was giving him a really bad involuntary hand job, he started going for the zipper of my jeans. I was scared, but I knew this day had to come sooner or later. I guess I was happy that I was about to get fingered. I didn't stop him. I can't say that he "slipped his fingers inside of me" because I assure you, it wasn't slippery. I wasn't turned on because I was nervous. Plus I hadn't been given much time to even get turned on. While he was fingering me I was still trying to concentrate on the hand job, but what he was doing hurt! His fingers felt huge and foreign in my preteen pussy. This certainly wasn't how I "fingered" myself! I think I let out a soft cry of pain, which he mistook for pleasure, and he proceeded to really ram his fingers in there like I was a 32-year-old porn star. Finally I stopped HJ'ing him and took his hand out of my vagina. He got pissed or insulted or embarrassed or whatever and stopped kissing me and turned on the light. I remember I looked at him and said "I'm sorry," and he said, "It's okay." We left the room and never saw each other again.

The sad thing is that in my demented brain, I picture that guy living with his wife today somewhere on Long Island and totally fingering her the same exact way. It hurts her, too, but she doesn't say anything. No one has ever said anything to him. It's like how everyone yes-yes'ed Britney Spears too much and told her it was OK to wear a scrunchie to the Grammys. In my brain, those asshole Long Island dudes are treated just like fucking celebrities, surrounded by wives and mothers and sisters who are too scared to tell them the truth. So next time you see your brother and it's in Long Island and he's being an asshole and his name is Eric, tell him he can't finger for shit.

HIGH
SCHOOL

AGE 14–18

NOT A LOSER ANYMORE

✶

SEPTEMBER 1993 • 9TH GRADE-AGE 14

DEAR DIARY,

I just can't take this anymore!!! The other day Jamie, Aimee, and Jan started with me because they thought I talked about them. Then they called me and apologized and said that Mikki told them all these things. Jan pushed me into a locker and it freaked me out. I can't believe Mikki would totally turn on me. I can never trust her again. I hope she gets it all back. I know that's bad to say but it's true. I kinda like Joe Meraita. He's friends with Butch and a skater dude. He found out that I liked him so now that's fucked. I really hate school. Syosset High sucks. I'm not doing well in kick line or in any of my classes. I just want to know what will become of me! I just want to find love. I don't ask for much. So why can't I have it just this once? My life really sucks. I'm going to see Juliana Hatfield on October 1st. I don't know what to do about dance classes. I know I'm bad. I'm bad at everything I do. Please let me be somebody and fall in love soon.

UPDATE · First week of high school and people already want to beat me up. Joe Meraita was a lanky skater kid with huge baggy pants and a different Blind T-shirt for every day of the week. He had bleached hair, sometimes dyed different colors, a big nose, and an even bigger personality. The dude was on fire! He had a million friends and liked bands that had cool names, like Bad Religion and Born Against. When I had a crush on him I used to call him and sing, "Twenty twenty twenty four hours to go, I want Joe Meraita."

NOVEMBER 1993 · 9TH GRADE-AGE 14

DEAR DIARY,
Two nights ago Leigh and I wanted to get drunk so we asked Brina to get us Zimas and she did. They didn't taste good. Getting drunk was boring too.

UPDATE · Brina was my neighbor who was older than us but not 21, so I don't know why we thought she'd be able to get us Zima, which was our preferred drink because I thought it tasted like Sprite. It didn't. Leigh and I sat on the curb in my neighborhood (I lived in a condominium) and tried to down the drink, but drinking is boring, especially when you're young. You need some kind of activity or drinking game or meal to get into it. It would have made more sense if it was a crew of us but it was just Leigh and I. We just wanted to feel what being drunk felt like. I vaguely remember faking drunk so that we could just go home.

Lesley: Do you remember when we drank Zima?
Leigh: Yeah. It sucked.

Remember how fucked up we used to get off Cisco?

Yes.

That was our shit.

Yes. That shit is crazy. Do you remember when we went to my parents' friend's party? It was like a lobster bake? I got fucking wasted there. I fell down the steps. That was maybe one of the drunkest nights of my life. I was drinking pineapple-infused vodka and smoking weed with my dad behind a tree but we used to get drunk on Cisco at Ezra's house with Freddy Capabianco. That shit seriously made you want to punch somebody or, like, hump somebody.

Yeah. It's cry, fuck, or fight. That's it. It takes you straight there, no detours.

Yeah—total crack juice.

It was good but it was no whippets.

Haha I know.

We got into whippets really late. It was, like, the highlight of my senior year.

They're fucking awesome. Seriously, that's my drug of choice.

You know what? We did them right. People are like, "Oh yeah, whippets. Get a can of whipped cream and suck on it." Oh no.

Fuck that! You need the balloons and the crackers and everything.

And the canister and the most specific kind of balloon. It can't just be any balloon.

Real thick. We used to do double dips.

Whatever! We used to take a bong hit, blow it in the balloon. and fill the balloon up with the cracker—essentially we were just making ourselves pass out.

So good.

PUNK ROCK GIRL

✶

DECEMBER 1993 • 9TH GRADE-AGE 14

DEAR DIARY,

Last night me, Ally, Deidre, Kim, and Missy Brennan all went to the Shoppe. They are all older than us and they are awesome. We had the best time! We all got ready at Missy's house and she drove us there. I met Justin Taylor and he called me. He gave me a sticker that says "Masturbation is yummy" and I put it on my backpack. Other than that, this vacation really sucks.

UPDATE • To think I actually had a sticker on my backpack that said, "Masturbation is yummy" when I was 14 gives me a case of the douche chills. Did my mom see that? Ewwwww. My poor father.

Justin Taylor was this kid I met at the teen club the Shoppe, and it seemed like his parents let him do whatever he wanted. My mom drove me to his house and we hung out and listened to mix tapes and talked about farting. He lives in

Brooklyn now, and sometimes I even see him riding his bike. Missy Brennan was this superhot, cool, older girl who was half Chinese and wore Freesia perfume from Bath and Body Works. Whenever I smell it, I smell sweet Missy Brennan with her beat-up Doc Martens and the cool college boyfriend she had who gave me a ride to Lollapalooza. I tried my ass off to locate her for this book but she's gone, poof, erased from the world i.e. probably living in Paris with a scruffy architect who loves her kids and runs a gallery called Fuck This or something equally amazing.

DECEMBER 1993 · 9TH GRADE-AGE 14

DEAR DIARY,
I hate my life. I hate myself. I hate having to repeat the same thing every day. I feel like we are all robots in this world. I am so sick of crying every day. I hate my family, I'm sick of being the bad one. I really need a love and someone to talk to and a reason to get up in the morning and a reason to stop hating myself.

UPDATE · Ever heard of Hugh Everett's "Many Worlds Interpretation of Quantum Mechanics"? It's that thing where they say there's a parallel universe for every decision you ever made.

In a parallel universe I was never hated in junior high. I went through it easily enough, was never the most popular but definitely not the most hated either. In this universe I grew up listening to Top 40 and never really caring about music because it held no sentimental value to me. It was something there just to distract me to have a minute of quiet, a minute to actually think or, rather, be without thought.

I would grow up and go to a state college and find a boring job one day where I'd sit in a cubicle and change into my Reeboks on the commute home to Queens. This is how I always pictured how my life would have turned out had my junior high school experience not been so traumatizing. So, every day I thank God I was miserable. Seriously. You have no idea what an opposite of everything you think you need and want will actually be. I'm so glad it was a nightmare. It could have been a lot worse, and sometimes, when I feel like I'm boring, I actually wish it were.

FEBRUARY 1994 · 9TH GRADE-AGE 14

DEAR DIARY,

I haven't written in so long because my room flooded but I went to the Roxy and met this kid Ruby. He's the drummer for the Warped Weeble Wobbles. He is the greatest—sophomore at BU, the smartest kid I have ever met. I cut my hair short. My life is so boring. All I do is drink coffee. I'm just waiting for something to happen. It seems that just a chain of negative events keeps taking place. If something good doesn't happen soon, I'm going to lose my mind. I don't give a shit about anything anymore. I'll smoke my Camel Lights, drink my coffee, and only surround myself with people who I find intellectually stimulating.

UPDATE · That last line was stolen from the alterna-teen classic *Reality Bites*, which had just come out. I obviously wanted to be a character in that movie because the person who wrote that was not me. The truth is I gave a shit about everything, too much of a shit. I never wanted to admit it because it stressed me out, and I have no idea why I didn't tell my diary as much. At that age you're so self-conscious you don't even let yourself know you're not a character in *Reality Bites*.

The Weebles were Long Island's jokey hardcore band, and this was the beginning of my long stint in the hardcore scene. We didn't really have so much of a punk scene because in Long Island, jock mentality overrides everything, even with the people who are supposedly anti-jock (I called this the punk years, though, because if you say "the hardcore years" it sounds like you were doing porn and freebasing—which I didn't do until much later).

Hardcore and punk are made up of kids who, for whatever reason, were outcasts at school. Half of them were weird smart kids who didn't fit in because they were weird and smart. The other half were just bad eggs who didn't fit in because they hated everyone and everything. I was the former, and so were a bunch of guys who were way older than me, like Mike "Ruby" Rubin and Bobby Eckstein.

FEBRUARY 1994 · 9TH GRADE-AGE 14

DEAR DIARY,
I was so happy when I came home from school because I had gotten a letter from Bobby. He is the

sweetest guy. I can't say I'm in love with him or any-thing because I hardly know him. I really look up to and respect Ruby but sometimes I wonder if he thinks I'm totally annoying or that it's ridiculous for us to talk on the phone. If there are two people on this planet I look up to it's Ruby and Sam Adamson. She is so cool and her opinion means so much to me. None of her friends talk to me anymore. Mikki is probably happy about that. I hate her more than anything. If anyone deserves hell it should be her. She's not worth wasting paper on. I got into another fight with Carrie. I don't really give a shit about her or anyone else for that matter. I've been treated like shit on a stick my whole life and I just don't give a fuck anymore. I hope I go to the city tomorrow. If not, I hope to see Bobby and Ruby.

UPDATE · Now, I know you're thinking, "What the fuck are 20-year-old men doing writing letters to a 15-year-old girl?" I don't know. They weren't gay, or slow (both are pro-fessors now), and if they were just doing it to get in my pants they certainly never tried. As weird as it sounds, I think we were all just friends and age didn't matter.

Sam Adamson was two grades older than me, and I totally looked up to her. She was down with the popular kids, but that never stopped her from dyeing her hair blue and making out with chicks, dancing on the cafeteria table and reading *Siddhartha* alone in the grass. She had a sticker on her car that said "STAY AWAKE" and claimed she would try anything once, just for the experience. She went to Bard College and became a historian/stripper. Today she lives in Amsterdam like it's no big deal.

MARCH 1994 · 9TH GRADE-AGE 15

DEAR DIARY,

Today as I came home from school I saw a car in the driveway. I walked in and there was Bobby and Ruby!! They were in my living room talking to my mom, which I thought would embarrass me but it didn't. We went to Ruby's house. It was fun! I love Bobby; he's too old for me though. I hate age and I hate school. Ahhhhhh I HATE MY LIFE!!!!

UPDATE · "I hate my life" is teen speak for "Things are going pretty good." The same way Garfield fans sarcastically scream "Aaaargh, Mondays," I was doing that thing where you're happy but you don't want to be gay about it so you say something like, "I hate age."

Coming home to see Bobby and Mike is one of my fondest memories. It's those little things that stick with you. Like the time you pretended to be asleep in the backseat and your dad carried you upstairs to bed.

I can still see them sitting in my living room. Bobby was about 5'3", had tiny little dreads (the Perry Farrell look was big) and a knit cap (before grunge made you barf). Ruby (Mike Rubin) was wearing a big chain wallet and corduroys and a plaid shirt—all animal friendly, what a hunk! They were the epitome of cool to me, and I was beaming. I introduced them to my mom, and Ruby said, "We're a little older than Lesley but don't worry, we're not pedophiles." It was the beginning of a lifelong friendship.

Bobby is 30 now, and he teaches psychology at the University of New Hampshire. Vanessa is his wife. She owns a flower shop.

Lesley: I'm calling because I wanted to ask you about when we first became friends. I was in 9th grade and you and Ruby were both in college . . .
Bobby: Um . . . I actually did think it was weird. I especially thought it was weird because my little brother is the same age as you.

Why were you guys bothering with such a young girl?
I think we were probably a little flattered that you had taken an interest in our band. It wasn't so much that you were really cool or anything, it's just that we were very uncool.

So you and Ruby never wanted to get with me? The thought of hooking up never crossed your mind?
You know what? No. There was a time after we became friends where I was confused about that a little bit.

Yeah, I had a huge crush on you.
Well, at the beginning I didn't think of you like that. I was also kind of young and I was so shy and awkward about that stuff. And also, less so now than then, I had a weird moral code.

What do you think you would have done if I had tried to hook up with you?
I have no idea. That's a great question but there was definitely a point where . . . I don't know if "crush" is the right word,

but I wondered if you were the girl who should've been my girlfriend.

DEAR DIARY,
I hate my father I hate my father I hate my father I
hate my father I hate my father I hate my father I
hate my father I hate my father I hate my father I
hate my father I hate my father I hate my father I
hate my father I hate my father I hate my father I
hate my father I hate my father I hate my father I
hate my father I hate my father I hate my father I
hate my father I won't waste any more paper on him.

UPDATE · My dad and I had some issues. I don't remember around what age they started. I think it could have been around my 12th birthday when I asked for cowboy boots instead of something more kidlike, like Nintendo. I was growing up and was getting girlier by the minute. Cowboy boots were in style that year. I think he didn't want me to get older and almost resented me for it. Sometimes I think he wanted me to be a boy, or at least remain his little pal forever. He used to bring me comic books. One year, I just stopped wanting them; you can't read Archies forever. I don't know if he was quite ready for that day.

So we argued a lot, and he was big and mean and when he got angry I was scared of him. I'll never forget the day I went into Manhattan with my neighbor. We weren't really allowed to go into the city by ourselves, and I knew that but asked him for a ride to the train station and he said yes. I thought that was a green light to go to the city and not get shit for it.

When I got home, my mother asked me where I had been, and when I told her, she was furious. I wasn't allowed to do that and didn't I know? Yes, but Dad gave me a ride. I guess my dad felt dumb at that moment and, in turn, started to rage.

I don't remember exactly where he hit me or for how long, but I do remember being on the floor and being kicked repeatedly.

I don't remember it happening in slow motion, like some people remember things. It wasn't slow. It wasn't like we were underwater. That's not what memory feels like.

Memory feels like flashes of light, like when you get your picture taken and you close your eyes from the brightness of the bulb. The lights were on in my bedroom. I felt exposed. It was quick and grainy and kept on happening even hours later, a throbbing feeling, like when you close your eyes supertight and you can sort of make out an image even though nothing is there.

My mom just walked away. She went into her room and closed the door. I remember thinking to myself as he punched me in the face and kicked me in the stomach, "You're too old for this." I was too old to be hit like that, I thought. But now I look back and I think I was always too old to be hit like that. It wasn't just a spanking. It was a thrashing.

After that incident we pretty much ignored each other for the duration of my high school years. When we ate dinner, my dad referred to me in the third person. "She just uses us," he would say.

We never hugged. During graduation or birthdays it was always awkward. I don't remember much more. Not concrete details at least. I remember losing my appetite at dinner. His fists pounding the table, making the plates jump. Maybe they were scared too.

Dads need to get over it and accept that their little buddy is a woman now and she's not going to tell him everything that happened at school or hang out with him all the time. Not for the next ten years anyway. If he can't get over that, you need to go to your room, scream into your pillow, put on the Bad Brains, and write in your diary.

I didn't want to talk to my dad specifically about this event because not even I have the balls big enough to go there. I did want to talk to my dad, however, and let him know that I wasn't going to hold back.

Lesley: I kind of don't want you to read the book.
Dad: That's not good.
Well . . . I mean . . . it's sort of like . . . read at your own risk? It's not good for you, but it's good for me. It's just, you know, embarrassing. I don't want either of my parents to read it.
Well, I don't really know what to say to that. It's kind of hard.
Do you want to read it?
I have always wanted to read and see your art, but most of the time you didn't want me to. When I did read it, it made me sick.
That's why I didn't give you stuff to read! If my art made you feel sick, that made me feel really bad. I didn't like being judged by my dad, hence me not showing you!
I understand. Don't get angry.
But that was such a weird thing you just said.
You told me you have questions for me but you don't want me to read it. How am I supposed to understand that? Think about that.
I can't imagine why you can't understand that. This is a compilation of all my diaries, so for me to have my parents read it, it's just, like, the cringe factor.
But it's also that your parents want to see your art.
Do you want to know about me having sex and doing drugs?
Um . . . if that's part of the story . . . I don't know. I'm talking

in a void here because I don't know what I'm talking about particularly. There are different kinds of art. The other day someone showed me a song, and I always look at the song and take it away from the first person and I always put it into "he, they, she, it" instead of "I," because those are always hard to read, just by the nature of the confessional. It's always easier to tell a story by putting it at a distance.

What are you talking about?

You're writing a diary, a confessional by nature it's "I," unless you fictionalize the thing, and if you fictionalize the thing then it becomes not what you intended but it also gives you a way to go over the top.

[*Sigh*] This isn't fiction. I just wanted to let you know so that it doesn't come as a shock to you that we had problems in our relationship when I was growing up. I wrote about this stuff in my diary, and it is also in the book.

OK, so now we're gonna share that with everybody else in the world?

Yes.

Right.

Another girl, somewhere in Minnesota, might be going through the same thing and feel the same way. Maybe if she reads this, she'll realize that she's not the only one who goes through this stuff.

Right. This is true. Then also I have to deal with lots of people who will look at me as the bad guy. I'm sure your mother probably comes off as Saint Joanne. So I have to consider that too.

Why would you think that my mom comes off as a saint?

You have no idea what my relationship is like with her.
I'm just reacting to the sentence you just said.
Dad, I don't want to hurt your feelings. It's my obligation to tell the truth, and it's very painful for me to have to do that and also to have to say this to you. I can't just not write about stuff because I'm afraid of hurting people's feelings.
You have to go for broke if that's what your art is. You can't be inhibited. I hear what you're telling me, and I'm not fighting with you, but it might not be the easiest thing in the world for me to deal with.
Right. I think that if anyone were to read this and judge you for it, then they are not someone you should really be friends with. I would hope also that it's obvious that I love you. I also love my life today, and I owe that to you and to mom. So even though we went through really hard times, it came out positive for me in the end.
OK. That's something. That's positive. I like hearing that. So what is it that you want to ask me, because I have to leave here soon?
I guess that's pretty much it.

APRIL 1994 · 9TH GRADE-AGE 15

DEAR DIARY,
Came back from Florida today. It was OK. Leigh talked to Stu Wildstein every day for hours. I don't know what's so great about him. I read her diary. I can't explain how I feel about Ruby. I know he doesn't love me the way I love him. Not really the same way I like Bobby because I don't know Bobby as well

and I'm totally making up what I want him to be in my head. I want to stay home this summer so bad. I really don't want to go to camp anymore.

UPDATE · Stu Wildstein was probably about the most Wild Stein you could ever imagine. He was tall and weird and had more charisma up his ass than David Lee Roth backstage at a David Lee Roth concert. But he was also suspiciously quiet, like the guy who killed the girl in *River's Edge*. Leigh always sat shotgun in his car and even occasionally got to play with the alligator he kept in his bathtub. Seriously. He had that. He had guns, a waterbed, and even a secret loft in his closet where certain neighborhood boys would hang out. That's right—straight boys would come to his house and fucking blow him! Stu was gay, but he said he was bi back when bi was just the opposite of hello. He wore a trench coat and had been kicked out of school in 11th grade for having guns and pot in his locker SEVEN YEARS before Columbine (nice try, Klebold). Even his death was cool. He crashed his motorbike going at about one million miles an hour (nice try, James Dean).

It was around this time I stopped being best friends with my best friend Leigh. She just got way cooler than me, and being friends with Stu didn't exactly hurt . . .

Lesley: I felt sad when we were in Florida and you talked to Stu the whole time so I read your diary.
Leigh: What did I write?
You wrote that you didn't know what to do because the

McSheffrey twins and Kim didn't like me.

Shit.

Why did we stop being BFFs for so long?

I think we broke up because I was puffing and thugging.

Yeah, I was really bad at smoking weed. I was megajealous of Beth I'm sure because you were BFF with her.

She was just down to kick it with boys every day, which is what I wanted. I had no use for girls then, and she was more like a dude.

Yeah. And plus I was bad at giving hand jobs, which, by the way, I hear you were the best at. You win the award. I think I was scared of the thugs, to be honest.

They were puppies. I won the hand-job award? Sweet. What about BJs?

I didn't get an answer for that one because Nate said he'd gotten too many BJs in his life.

Ha!

I think really what I was most upset about was that I felt abandoned by you in 9th grade. Jan Graham wanted to beat me up, and I felt like I had no back from you. We started to drift apart and I tried to talk to you but you just weren't having it. Then I was just, like, Fuck it. I guess I thought I embarrassed you because I dressed weird and not like a thug. I thought, Even though I dress like this, Leigh will still stay true because she knows what's up because you were the bestest friend I ever had. So when I was wrong I just felt sad and stupid. So I guess my first question is, Why did you abandon me in 9th grade?

Oh Les, it was never about you, and I totes never wanted to

abandon you. I definitely never felt embarrassed by you. I just got selfish and wanted to get high and hook up with boys. I kinda felt like you thought the boys were lame and that I got lame.

I didn't like the way you were changing because we had been into the Beastie Boys and *Wayne's World*, and then suddenly you were over it. Shit, I'm STILL into *Wayne's World*.

I felt I was making the wrong decision and probably was but felt compelled to and you were a reminder that I was choosing poorly, then and now.

When I started chilling in 11th, I understood the appeal. Those guys were all really funny.

It was really fun and very intoxicating. It was a lot of ego stroking, which is hard to fight.

I always thought I was a weirdo you didn't want to know for a while but then I did drugs in 11th and got cool.

You came to the dark side, so I didn't have to hide.

APRIL 1994 • 9TH GRADE-AGE 15

DEAR DIARY,

You will never believe what happened. I MET MIKE D!!!! I said, "I love you," and gave him a hug. I even cried. It was gay but I don't care. Liz Phair was amazing and so were the Raincoats. Kurt Cobain died and it's sad I guess but I had the best night ever!! The Beastie Boys are also playing a show at the Academy. Today for the first day in a really long time I feel happy. I know it has to do with Ruby and Bobby. They really have changed my life. Every time I talk to

each of them I like that one a little bit more. They are really making me happy. I just hope something doesn't fuck it up . . .
PS KILL YOUR TELEVISON!

APRIL 15, 1994 · 9TH GRADE-AGE 15

DEAR DIARY,
I had fun on Monday with Mikey C; I haven't spoken to him in three days. I'm not mad, just upset. I wish I never met them. Why do I want them to like me so bad? Mikey C seemed a little bit distant on Monday. Bobby was really cute. Why do I feel this way? I'm definitely going crazy. Oh yeah, mom found out about the city. Big fucking deal. I cut school and hung out with them. Why am I torturing myself over this? Leigh is gone, I have no one.

UPDATE · These guys were seniors, getting ready to graduate, and I was still young and silly. They thought I was cool, which got me off because I thought they were so cool, but at the end of the day, they were still older, had been through more, and it was kind of weird.

WEIRDLY AWESOME, that is!
Let's face it; having older friends is fun. Besides them being able to drive you to all the cool happenings, they can teach you the unspoken etiquette that goes with being in high school. The kind of stuff only learned by experience, like knowing that you can't call shotgun until everyone is outside the diner. Ruby taught me why people are vegetari-

ans, health and environmental reasons that had nothing to do with loving animals. Bobby taught me that you shouldn't try to get into hardcore shows for free, you should pay because it's just kids putting it together and if I wanted to steal I should steal from the man, not DIY places. They taught me how you should always punch someone back harder than they punched you even if they're kidding, and how you NEVER tell anyone if you get an STD no matter what and how, outside of herpes and AIDS, STDs aren't really a big whup. Most of them are just a few pills or a blast of liquid nitrogen. The rules of cool were written by seniors, so make sure you befriend them and be careful not to get raped!

PS When they live in another town you get extra-credit cool points because it makes you seem more mysterious.

APRIL 1994 • 9TH GRADE-AGE 15

DEAR DIARY,

I guess I really can't tell whether Bobby has feelings for me. Sometimes I think it will work but then again, we are just great friends. I don't know what to do. I guess nothing is my only choice. Me, Leigh, Marisa, Mikey C, and Bobby all went to the movies yesterday. It was fun but a little awkward. Ruby told me I was his BF and that made me happy. Other than that I have nothing to look forward to.

UPDATE • This setup with the older kids was perfect because I could have these innocent nothing crushes on them and they'd never take advantage of it. Most girls were into horses. I was into old guys. They were training wheels for real boys in the real world, which I would get to soon enough. For the record, I don't recommend this. The odds of finding cooler, older guys to hang out with who have no ulterior motives are about 1 in 100. Today I almost exclusively date guys who look like they're 15 because I never got to date them when I really was that age. Like my boyfriend now, who looks like Doogie Howser if Doogie Howser were a fag. Oh wait, Doogie Howser is a fag.

MAY 1994 • 9TH GRADE-AGE 15

DEAR DIARY,
I hate my father. Bobby doesn't like me. I better be able to stay home this summer. I tried to kill myself.

UPDATE • "Trying to kill myself" consisted of scraping at my wrists with a pair of safety scissors that were so dull all they did was rouge up my skin a bit. No blood at all. Then I tried to raise the bar by drowning myself in my own teardrops. That didn't work either. My ideal scenario was to kill myself, make everyone feel terrible about not making me happy, torture the universe, and then come back from the grave saying, "All right. You learned your lesson. You better appreciate the shit out of me from now on."

Doesn't work. Killing yourself because you think your friends and family could do more to make you happy is like blowing up someone's country with a nuclear bomb because you heard a rumor that someone there is a dick.

You get way more out of scream-crying and slamming your door as hard as you can.

MAY 1994 · 9TH GRADE-AGE 15

DEAR DIARY,

I'm staying home this summer and working at Crestwood Day Camp. I went to the Beastie Boys concert last night it was amazing. I danced onstage with Luscious Jackson. I had the best time except Ruby, Bobby, and all of them won't talk to me because they say I embarrassed them by dancing onstage, they haven't called me yet.

MAY 1994 · 9TH GRADE-AGE 15

DEAR DIARY,

Bobby called me and apologized. Saturday night Marisa and me were supposed to go to the UN but Stu and Leigh dicked us and now Leigh and I are in a fight. I'm sick of this kinda shit. I don't care. She is being so immature. Sunday I went to the Right Track Inn to see the Weebles play. After, I went to Bobby's house. I LOVE Bob. We went to the beach with their annoying friends and Bobby and I just sat and snuggled in the car on the way back. He doesn't like-like me though. I have to face reality. Marisa's mom picked us up. I swear I'm never going anywhere with that girl again. She's weird.

UPDATE • Marisa was a really nice girl who just wasn't right in the head. When we were younger she was years ahead of everyone else. I never looked up to her, just envied her maybe. But it was hard to be jealous of Marisa because she just loved all her friends so much. She was always nice and fun and wanted to invite me everywhere. I even went to Florida with her and her family on their vacation.

As we entered high school, Marisa got kind of strange. I feel bad saying this about her because she's dead now, but she went from junior-high darling to very clingy, needy chick almost overnight. Suddenly snowy white hair was dyed black and blue. Her puffy winter coat was swapped for a very provocative-looking cloak. She even changed her name from Marisa to Faith. Legally. It was hard for me to catch on.

I loved her. We all loved her, but when she started showing me blisters on her legs from melted-candle-wax sex acts (she told me she was a dominatrix after school), things got a little too heavy for me. We were only 15!

The very last time I saw her was when we were 17. She just kind of appeared in the parking lot one day after school. We talked about how we had both gotten into going to raves and doing drugs. She said, "Wanna come over? My parents are away." I guess we had all heard at that point that Marisa was bisexual (Leigh told me), and I'd be lying if I said I didn't notice the gay little twinkle she had in her eyes. I was definitely curious and nervous and excited by the prospect of doing weird stuff at her house. So I did.

We went back to her house and put a bottle of K in the oven to bake so we could get lovely. (Keep in mind that I'm skipping ahead to 11th grade here. In 7th grade I tried pot a few times but didn't get into drugs until 3 years later. After punk. During rave.) We got high and ran around for a while just being silly. She whipped out a Polaroid and took pictures of me in my bra. I'm sure there was some blushing, but drugs do a good job of wiping out the shy factor. When she turned to me and said, "Do you want to take a bath?" I knew she meant, "Do you want to take a bath together?" Maybe I was curious to see how far we would take it, how far I would go. Plus, Leigh told me that she Frenched Marisa the previous summer, and maybe I was even a little jealous. If Leigh could make out with a girl, then I sure as hell could. It's funny to look back and see that having gay sex with Marisa was based on the competition I had with my best friend. I said yes to taking a bath. I said yes to all of it.

We both took off our clothes and got into the tub. She had been on antidepressants, so her once-long body that curved as gently as a white ribbon was now thick and pasty, as if her body itself had no memory of what it once was. It became a blank slate, something very foreign to me and even to Marisa. She was not the bikini-wearing blow-job queen I had known and had hoped my first lesbian experience would be with. Now she had both nipples pierced and fleshy arms that were reaching out and begging me to hold her. I obliged.

After the small hug-and-kiss session, she started washing my boobs. I wasn't horny, but I liked what was going on. Just because it made me feel so worldly and adult. "At least I'll have something to write about now," I figured. By then the K had sort of worn off, and the round, bubble-esque feeling had faded into the starchy, rude awakening of WTF?

We made out a little bit and had this awkward thing where she kind of went down on me in the tub but she couldn't breathe underwater and the shifting of positions had proved scary when I almost slipped and broke my neck. Water and sexual activity don't mix. That's why we evolved out of the ocean and became land dwellers 420 million years ago. So we moved it to the couch.

I couldn't come. I wanted to, if only to get it over with toward the end, but I just could not let go and get comfortable with the fact that Marisa was eating me out. I even asked her to put the porn channel on just to move things along, but she was all, "My parents might find out." What?!?! Now I definitely wouldn't be able to come. I was so mind-boggled that she was concerned with, of all things, her parents finding out about her watching porn?

After about an hour I gave up. I faked it and pulled up my pants. It's not that it didn't feel good, it did. It's just that sometimes, that's not all that counts. Maybe that's the day I learned orgasms were more mental than physical.

As I zipped my fly and reality kicked in, I kind of freaked. If we were a real couple, I would've been the dude-type figure at this point. I needed to leave her house stat. She started crying a little bit and told me how much I meant to her and how much she loved me. I loved her too. We were old friends. But now, old friends who had just done it. It doesn't matter what gender you are, having sex with friends is some tricky biz. As I ran out the door I left her quietly sobbing on her parents' black leather couch. Their house was an empty McMansion, devoid of personality. Marisa was the only thing that added the flavor. I chain-smoked my way home and wondered if this meant I was gay and if so, how would I tell my parents? I drew up scenarios in my head where I would have to wear a tux to the prom. Couldn't I be the girl? I couldn't. No matter how roly-poly she got, Marisa would always be prettier than me. Later I just shrugged the experience off and laughed about it with my friends, or even later in college, I'm sure it was something I bragged about.

When I think of Marisa, I never think of her sitting on that leather couch crying and begging me not to leave. I think of how she was in middle school, sexy and sly. Silly and crazy. I think of her red cowboy boots. I think of her singing along to "Joyride" by Roxette. I think of the time she told me she was adopted and how it kind of made me wish I had been adopted too. I never think of her pierced nipples or her new name. And only recently did I have to associate her with her very own funeral after she died of a heroin overdose. Now when I think about her, I also have to think about what went wrong and what if I had done something different.

May 1994 · 9th Grade-Age 15
DEAR DIARY,
I wish I never met any of the Weebles. I hate my life and there is something inside of me that refuses to come out no matter how hard I cry and I can't take it anymore. I am going to have to try anything to get this out of me.

UPDATE · The problem here was not that I hated the Weebles or any of these cool, older kids. The problem was I was totally out of my fucking league. I couldn't hang. I knew it was just a matter of time before one of them turned to the emperor and said, "Dude, you have no clothes on," and then everyone stared at my bush and I would be all, "Yeah. I know. Sorry you guys."

If I had a time machine I would go back and inject myself with Get Over It Juice.

July 1994 · Summer-Age 15
DEAR DIARY,
These two girls, Charlene and Darlene, started hanging out with the Weebles. Ruby said that Charlene liked Mikey C but now Darlene is going out with him. I hate them both. They're both bitches and I'll admit that I'm jealous of them being friends with the Weebles. Mikey C totally dicked me. I really hope Bobby thinks of me as being better friends than he is with them. I hope Charlene really did like Mikey C because now it's just a HA HA in her face. Fuck you Mikey. Fuck you Charlene and Darlene.

UPDATE · Darlene and Charlene, both beautiful, had the kind of cute hardcore-girl look that every girl in the scene seemed to try and adopt but failed. Darlene, half Cuban, half trashy Long Island, was short and olive colored with huge green eyes and the kind of butt that seemed to have a life of its own. She used to wear tank tops over T-shirts and stand on the side of the stage and dance while the mosh pit below would be a pulsating war zone of teenage acne, bloody teeth, and big fat magic-markered X's ("an X on your hand means you're in command" AKA you don't drink or do drugs) on pumped fists that were still pumping even days after the show had ended.

Charlene was like a slightly altered version of Darlene. It worked that their names rhymed. Charlene had short, boy-cut hair, same as Darlene but hers was bleached blond. Through the years Charlene would shave her head or dye it blue or poppy red, but she always looked hot. She was really into cars and boys and then, later, drugs. They were best friends and pals with all the guys and danced to hardcore music in sync with one another, shrugged up shoulders and heads bopping along as if the music were written solely for them.

I later became great friends with both of them, but during this time I just thought they were the worst. I was used to being the only girl, and I loved being young and cute and showered with attention. Of course it was too good to last. I was threatened by not one but two cute girls who seemed to be stealing my thunder. I had no choice but to deal with it. I did a lot of sulking alone in my bedroom.

They used to write in this big journal that they passed back and forth writing gay things like "The world will explode in 2000" and all the songs they'd ever used on a mix tape. Oh who am I kidding? Even their "gay" journal was amazing.

WHY CAN'T I GET A BOYFRIEND?

*

SEPTEMBER 1994 · 10TH GRADE-AGE 15

DEAR DIARY,

I saw this kid at a sweet sixteen who goes to my school: Christian. He is sooooo cute. Very Vermont, J. Crewish. I'm sure nothing will happen because 1) I hardly ever see him and 2) I'm sure we have nothing in common. I love thinking about him though. Tom bleached his hair and it looks cute. Ryan has been nicer and has been paying more attention to me. Hmmm . . . three guys. I'm sure nothing will happen with any of them. It's Saturday night and I'm doing homework. The reason why Tom never called was because he never got any of the messages. He's 20 years old!

UPDATE · Ryan was the bass player for Silent Majority but he pussied out. Tom was the singer of Vision of Destruction who was out of my league. Christian was an überpreppy kid who wasn't feeling me. It gets a little confusing here because I had crushes on basically every boy I saw. All they needed to do was be kind of cute and maybe smile at me once.

I liked Christian because I was totally obsessed with the idea of having a *Pretty in Pink* kind of romance. You know, a girl from the wrong side of the tracks gets a "Richie" to fall in love with her, but I wasn't from the wrong side of the tracks. I just pretended like I was. I even had a total Andie outfit, complete with pearls and some kind of vintage lace doily dress and Doc Martens. However, just like "Blaine" from *Pretty in Pink* was a "major appliance," Christian wasn't just a boy to me. He was a religion.

SEPTEMBER 1994 · 10TH GRADE-AGE 15

DEAR DIARY,

Today was not a good day with Christian. He doesn't know who I am but he knows that I like him. How horrible! I bet Carrie told his friends. You can't trust anybody. I'm not angry but I feel a little bit stupid. I hope tomorrow is better.

OCTOBER 1994 · 10TH GRADE-AGE 15

DEAR DIARY,

Another terrible day with Christian. I shouldn't even bother with him because nothing will come out of it. If anything, it would just be that he's flattered that a girl likes him. Why me?

OCTOBER 1994 • 10TH GRADE-AGE 15

DEAR DIARY,

Today was not a good day. I got ink all over my favorite pair of jeans—on the butt! Christian totally avoids me. My brace broke. I am going to talk to him tomorrow no matter what. We'll see what happens.

OCTOBER 1994 • 10TH GRADE-AGE 15

DEAR DIARY,

I swear, I really wanted to talk to him but I didn't see him alone all day.

OCTOBER 1994 • 10TH GRADE-AGE 15

DEAR DIARY,

Yesterday I saw Rancid/Avail/Queers at the Wetlands. It was awesome. Christian probably hates those bands. I think it's weird that Mikey C is going out with Darlene. I saw the fanzine last night and the section that I wrote was in but only the part where I called up different musicians and asked them what their first concert was. It looks pretty cool.

OCTOBER 1994 • 10TH GRADE-AGE 15

DEAR DIARY,
Today I said "Hi" to Christian in the hall.

OCTOBER 1994 • 10TH GRADE-AGE 15

DEAR DIARY,
Today I finally spoke to Christian. He was avoiding

me all day. Then Lauren from kick line came up to me and said that he was mad because his friend made these plans for Saturday night and didn't even tell him. So then I saw him and I'm like, "Chris, can I talk to you?" So we were talking and he just said he was pissed because we hardly knew each other and that he wasn't mad at me. I just said, "People have been making things really weird for me," and he's like, "Me too but it's not us, it's the people around us." Not much was really said after that. I hope this blossoms into a friendship.

OCTOBER 1994 · 10TH GRADE-AGE 15

DEAR DIARY,

Dear Me,

If he can't like you for who you are or what you wear then he's not even worth it. You have to be proud of yourself and proud of your individuality. You go to a school full of clones. You have always been known to stand out so don't let that reputation die down. Be in a good mood and be happy about how you look and what you're wearing and who cares what he thinks. You would never be able to talk to him anyway if he were to be like that. You are yourself and not what anyone else makes you out to seem. Maybe he likes you.

Love,

Me

UPDATE · Girls need to send out one simple look and leave it at that. If he doesn't come over to talk to you, DROP IT. All you're doing is humiliating yourself.

I had been playing phone tag with Christian for a while. He was hard to reach because he's like a big production guy on movie sets and is really busy. I am wet now just thinking about it. About how busy he is. Would you believe me if I said that his voice even sounded hot over the phone? The longer it took for me to get in touch with Christian, the more I wanted to talk to him. To date him. To make out with him on the lacrosse field. To pee on him in the shower. Just kidding. But it's fucked up how easy it is to want something just because you can't get it. I'm not even single and I haven't seen this kid in over 10 years. SO WHY DO I WANT TO FUCK HIM? Christian was busy and told me he'd call me back later, so I proceeded to wait by the phone until he did, all the while rubbing my temples and sending telepathic messages of love to him.

Lesley: I had a huge crush on you in high school and I wrote a lot about you.
Christian: High school is an impressionable time of your life.
That is true.
What did you want to know?
Why didn't you have a crush on me?
That's a question I don't think I can answer.
Are you married?
I am about to be engaged very shortly.
Oh.

Dear Diary

DEAR DIARY,

I saw Brad and Ryan last night. I think I like Brad
better but I'm not sure how he feels about me. Ryan
and I were flirting a lot more. Then I had a dream
about Christian. I don't know what to do. This
morning at 8 o'clock a blue car pulled up to my
house and started honking really loud. Finally a girl
came out and screamed "I HATE YOU!" at my front
door. I called Ryan and he didn't call me back. I am
a nice person now. I don't know who I like, Ryan,
Brad, or Christian.

Ryan	Brad	Christian
- Hot	- V. cute	- V. cute
- Dumb	- Smart	- Book smart
- In a band	- Plays the	- Plays hockey/
- Sweet	drums	soccer
- A little cheesy	- Skater	- Shy
- Doesn't talk	- Sweet	- Preppy
that much	- Talks a lot	- Likes
		Candlebox
		- Doesn't talk
		to me

UPDATE · Hold on. A car came up to my house and someone got out and screamed, "I hate you"?!? How did I just
glance over that like I was saying someone dropped a gum
wrapper near my friend's house? George Bush doesn't even

have people doing that to his house. Even rapists and pedophiles don't get that. Actually that's not true, they might get that, but I was just a sassy teenager. I never found out what happened with that and who did it, and for some reason I cannot fathom even to this day, I didn't care. The only one of these boys who matters is Brad, and even that was just for three weeks.

NOVEMBER 1994 · 10TH GRADE-AGE 15

DEAR DIARY,
Tonight I saw Silent Majority, Doc Hopper, Garden Variety, and Big Sniff. I had the best time! I am so attracted to Ryan but three guys like me. RT, Chris, and this kid Dave with blond hair. I like Brad and Ryan. Life sucks right?

UPDATE · Most of these shows were in Manhattan at places like CBGBs, the Wetlands, ABC No Rio, and Coney Island High. They would be all-ages matinees on a Sunday, so we could get there and back by train and not have to lie to our parents. Sometimes they would be at the Northport Pipeline, a Long Island skate park, and sometimes at the Y, but those places aren't as cool to name-drop.

Chris and Dave with the blond hair are irrelevant, but RT (AKA Artie) at the time was the king of the hardcore scene. He booked every band, was funny, mean, and obnoxious, wrote a really great column in a hardcore zine, had great moshing skills, had a punk history of having a junkie dad and dropping acid in high school, and had even lived on his own since he was 16. I didn't have a crush on him. We remained friends and still talk all the time. I hooked him up with *Vice* and now he writes more stuff than I do.

JANUARY 1995 · 10TH GRADE-AGE 15

DEAR DIARY,

Ahhh! Julian called me tonight! Can you believe that? I can't believe that I am writing in my diary about how a 24 year old just called me and I am 15! Does he think I'm 16? Probably. He didn't have to call me, he had no reason to but he did and I love it!

UPDATE · Julian was tall and pale, but his face turned bright red when he sang in his band Crisis Overload. He had a shaved head and wore zip-up hoodie sweatshirts. He was also a bus driver, which made me feel conflicted because at that time I was still taking the bus to school. I'm sure I even asked him what it was like to drive a bus and if it was hard. I mean, I rode the bus every day and often wondered how one decided to become a bus driver and if they found it hard to make right turns. It seemed like such a different kind of life. Where do bus drivers come from?

I was 15. He was 24. That's not a date. That's illegal. He was so cute and cool and punk, I wonder how he thought it was OK to ask me out? The date sucked. We went to the movies but for some reason only wanted to see something at this specific art-house theater, and the only thing playing there was this lesbian drama called *Bar Girls*. Not a good movie, even by lesbian standards. If that wasn't awkward enough, I had a really bad cough during the entire movie. I was coughing so much that the dyke sitting next to me started giving me dirty looks. I didn't blame her. The cough was so annoying it was basically picking a fight with her. When he dropped me off I just jumped out of his van and said good-bye and ran to my door as quickly as possible because I didn't want to cough in his face.

I tried to contact Julian for this book, but he wasn't having it. Today he sings in a band called Miranda Rights, and according to Artie, he is still a bus driver. I e-mailed him twice and even called him, but his phone was disconnected. I was sad because who knows? We could've been soul mates (JK).

MARCH 1995 · 10TH GRADE-AGE 16

DEAR DIARY,
My dream is to be a wonderful writer. For now on, I am going to write and write as much as possible with details so exact that the person reading can actually come alive in the story. I can't wait!

UPDATE · "For now on": Writing in your diary doesn't make you a writer any more than fucking a lot doesn't make you a fucker. You have to get published to make it real, and a book of diary entries does not count.

MARCH 1995 · 10TH GRADE-AGE 16

DEAR DIARY,
The only thing I can think about is Brad. What is going to happen? I love this but there is still that lit-

tle feeling inside me that things won't work out the way I plan it to. I really don't want to become a "girlfriend" and I would like to explain this to him but I don't think he would understand. He didn't even understand *Pulp Fiction*! I don't want to be known as "Brad's new girlfriend." I just want to be known as Lesley. I don't want to turn into one of those girls who just laugh at what their boyfriends say and sit on their laps and act all stupid and girlish. Fuck that—I hope that's not how it turns out.

UPDATE • Listening to all that feminist punk really ruined what I thought a boyfriend was supposed to be. I wanted to be molested but respected. I wanted to be affectionate but not a stereotypical "girlfriend," because I thought that wasn't punk. I loved boys so much but desperately wanted to hate all men. It was all I had to latch on to. My identity as a hardcore girl in the scene was so blurry. It was like we didn't exist if we weren't cute and subservient but being cute and subservient to me felt like a nonexistence. I wanted to be that way—cute and quiet and a fan of all the bands—but it wasn't right. For starters, I wasn't that cute. And I wasn't quiet, I was loud and obnoxious. I couldn't just be a fan of the bands, because all the bands were really shitty.

I hadn't gone all the way but fantasized about it all the time. I was angry about how scared I was of the crazy things I wanted to do, but admitting that is something teenagers do not do. I don't even think most adults do it. I had a lot of plans to live a certain kind of way, like sing in a band and travel around and learn that saltwater trick where you get free sodas. At the end of the day I just didn't really have the balls for any of it. Balls aren't something you're born with. Maybe small ones are, but the big ones are acquired by facing your fears and doing it anyway.

APRIL 1995 · 10TH GRADE-AGE 16

DEAR DIARY,
I've decided that I really want to move to Holland when I'm older.

UPDATE · I liked Amsterdam back then because my English teacher gave us an article about how drugs and prostitution were legal there and the country was thriving. I was all, "See America? In your face!" When I went to Amsterdam with Leigh in my 20s, we slept on a mattress in a hostel and got high at the Doors café. Then we walked around and wanted to eat everything we saw. I swear to God. When I was looking at Anne Frank's house and the Van Gogh museum all I could think was how delicious they would be if they were chocolate. I even caught myself staring at these wooden clogs Leigh bought as a souvenir for her nana and thinking, "Mmmm. Tasty."

When we went back to the hostel every American tourist was stoned and zoned and watching MTV, and we were like, "Fuck this shit."

APRIL 1995 • 10TH GRADE-AGE 16

DEAR DIARY,

Last night Brad was supposed to come over but things got screwed up and I ended up going to the stupid boring show. I don't know what the deal is. When we're apart he wants to be with me but when it's time for us to be together things get all screwed up. Sometimes I think I might be blowing things out of proportion and he really doesn't like me as much as I like him.

UPDATE • You know that feeling. When you like a boy but then he starts to like you and you stop liking him. That happened to me a lot. I didn't want to belong to any club that would have me as a girlfriend.

APRIL 1995 • 10TH GRADE-AGE 16

DEAR DIARY,

I'm getting really frustrated about the fact that Brad hasn't kissed me yet. Does he even like me at all? I feel both ways because also the thought of calling him right now kind of makes me sick. What happened to spring and warmth and love? It's still so cold outside and so are my feelings about him right now. I don't know how I feel about Brad. Why is this happening?

APRIL 1995 • 10TH GRADE-AGE 16

DEAR DIARY,

Well Brad and I kissed last night. The first time was

under his covers, then in the car a lot. His mouth is just so much bigger than mine and then he called me and was like, "Did you have a good time tonight?" And I was like, "Yeah. Did you?" And he was like, "Yeah. We kissed." OH GOD. I just really don't love

him. I'm just so sick of everybody. Even though I act all tough it's really not good or fun to have enemies at all. It always seems like someone hates me and not Emily or Lydia and isn't it funny how I just kissed this boy and all I can think about is who hates me and moving to California? The other night me, Lydia, and Emily got totally pissed drunk and I puked so much.

UPDATE · I called up Brad and remembered immediately why we weren't soul mates. Brad and I have no chemistry, and where there's no chemistry, there's no sparks. I could tell by his voice that he was still hot, but I was running low on care juice while he seemed to be drunk on the stuff. He teaches 3rd grade in Brooklyn and is still insanely good-looking, but when all I wanted to do was talk about me, he kept changing the subject to seeing *Pulp Fiction* for the first time and how that changed how he felt about all movies forever and the importance of independent meow meow meow zzzzzzzzzzz. This from the guy I fell out of love with because he didn't even get the movie.

Lesley: Hey Brad! Still teaching?
Brad: Yeah. I just hang out with my little punks.
Oh that makes it sound cooler.
Yeah it's good, I'm still very passionate about art and music so it's a good outlet for me to do something where I make money and I'm doing something meaningful in the world.
Why did it take you so long to bust a move on me?
I guess at that time in my life I was very consumed with other people's perspective of me. Especially in the weird high school–ish sort of hardcore-punk scene.
So if you made out with me it wouldn't be punk?
No it would've looked great on my machismo record to have made out with as many girls as possible . . . I guess?
So what the fuck are you talking about?
To me it was more like we were seeing each other. A close friendship but maybe just a little more than that? But in terms of being committed . . . I just don't think it was like that.

MAY 1995 · 10TH GRADE-AGE 16

DEAR DIARY,

It always seems that no matter how nice I am, I'm always ugly to someone else. No matter how pretty I try to look, I'm still the same ugly person. Someone is always disliking me and I always do something wrong. My whole life this has been following me. Nothing ever stays right. I wonder what I've done. I wish I knew.

UPDATE · Do boys go through this phase of unintelligible self-hatred and low self-esteem? With girls it does pass, although it's something we hold on to, well into adulthood. I don't feel this way about myself today, but I certainly haven't forgotten what this feels like, either. One thing that helped build up an immunity to mean jokes was hanging out with hardcore dudes for so many years. Snapping on people just became part of the daily routine.

When people point out how much I look like Harmony Korine I can just laugh (he does look kind of like a pretty Jewish girl in some pictures). If you don't know how to laugh at yourself, then you don't know how to laugh at anything.

JULY 1995 · SUMMER-AGE 16

DEAR DIARY,

I'm in another fight with Emily and it hurts. It's like, I totally love her and all but there's just something . . . she's so depressing and sometimes makes me feel so bad. She also talks shit on all these people but then would rather hang out with them than me and everybody loooves her. I know when we go our separate ways we won't be friends anymore. I just can't picture us being friends forever. I guess it's just so hard because Leigh was a great best friend for a while and it's so hard to forget that. For me at least. I love it how deep inside and maybe not even so deep, everybody just looks out for themselves and although I probably don't realize it, I do too. It just seems that I make myself so vulnerable and like, everyone is always out to get me. Why is it always me?

UPDATE · Emily Aronofsky was a year older than me, and we went to the same school. We realized we were meant to be friends when she saw me wearing a backpack at the Roxy one night. She was wearing a backpack too. Then I saw her in a Jawbreaker T-shirt in the cafeteria, and then I saw her at the PWAC (People With AIDS Coalition, where a lot of bands played). One day we realized that we both hated everyone equally, and that was it. Friends for life. We would laugh over which loser we would use for rides to get to the next hardcore show and then ditch them once we got there. If Leigh was my Enid from *Ghost World*, Aronofsky was the Nicky to my Pammy (*Times Square*). She introduced to me the best bands, borrowed my favorite fanzines and never gave them back, got the crush on the drummer when I wanted the singer. We were total fucking homeys. Things started to go awry, as most adolescent friendships do, and we lost touch for a while, but now we are homeys again! Today Emily works at MTV and looks exactly like she did when she was 16. Skinny, pretty, long eyelashes, and a cute Jewie butt. She traded in her XXL jeans and "Castrate Rapists" shirt for H&M gear and straightened her long, reddish brown curly hair. Other than that she looks the same and pretty much acts the same, which is awesome.

Lesley: I remember that day in Waldenbooks when I called you a junkie.
Emily: WHAT?
I went to visit you at work right and you and I were sort of on the outs because you had other friends and you told me you had tried heroin and to be honest I think I was almost kind of jealous because I wanted to try new things with you and I secretly wanted to try that.
Sadly makes sense.
So I went to visit you at work and we got into a fight there. I yelled at you and called you a "fucking junkie" and stormed out.
How dramatic. Oh my God, another one I remember and I still feel bad about to this very day . . .
Tell me.
. . . When I took your dad's beeper. There were a ton of people at your house and we found a beeper and I took it. You said I could and it turns out it was your dad's so I dropped it off at your house and THIS I'LL NEVER FORGET your mom was furious at me when she met me at the front door. I was so upset so I wrote her a note!

My dad had a beeper because he was a liquor salesman, but I liked it because it made him look like a dealer. We were both mad you stole it. The whole family was!

I felt so bad. Honestly to this day it still makes me sad because it makes me feel like a total dirtbag addict. Do you think your mom is still mad? Tell her I'm sorry again.

I'm surprised my dad didn't yell at you. A lot of people stole shit from my house.

Really?

Lydia and Artie stole tapes. My whole tape case.

NO!

And then Artie gave me a ride somewhere and I was like, why is my tape case back here? Haha.

Hahaha.

It's so funny. He stole my Tilt tape. Then I wanted to hear Tilt because I hadn't heard it in so long because he fucking stole it so I asked him to put it on.

I'm laughing so hard right now.

SEPTEMBER 1995 · 11TH GRADE – AGE 16

DEAR DIARY,

I don't really like Emily very much anymore. I really want to but she's always complaining about something! I hate to say it but as soon as I drive, I might have no friends and that's fine with me!

SEPTEMBER 1995 · 11TH GRADE – AGE 16

DEAR DIARY,

Last night Doc Hopper and Weston stayed at my

house. Pretty fucking cool. The dudes from Weston are sooo funny we had an awesome time. It's weird, every time a band stays here, Tovah and Emily always end up hooking up in one way or another but not me. I just feel like a big geek sometimes. As much as I hate to say it, I hate punk rock.

UPDATE · I hated punk in Long Island because it wasn't punk. It was high school hardcore sXe (straight edge) jocks pretending to give a shit. All we did was go to shows, go to diners, make fun of people, and talk shit. I guess that's all I do now, but I was addicted to heroin, what do you want me to do? Go to bars? Anyway, back then I was craving a little more adventure than the life of a clean and sober 27-year-old in a long-term relationship. Uh-oh. Things are about to get phat ...

RAVER GIRL

DECEMBER 1995 · 11TH GRADE-AGE 16

DEAR DIARY,
Oh my goodness, drugs really do work. Um, hello Special K, crystal meth, E . . . ? This 4-day weekend was a nonstop roller coaster. Probably met the crush of all crushes and a million more. I went to visit Lydia at school and she wanted to take me to a rave with her new friends who are so awesome. I wanted to go to the party but when I first got there I was kind of bored. Then Susan gave me an E pill and suddenly it was like I was walking on a cloud. It was soooo phat. There were some embarrassing moments after I took the crystal, like kissing Lydia and eating candy . . . it's all too much. I can't talk about it. It seems like this is not my diary. When I read back it's all about crushes—how sad.

UPDATE · The first time I ever did Special K, crystal meth, and ecstasy was all on the same night. The night of my first rave. The K felt like being in a bubble. I wasn't in a "K hole" or anything, just a weird round feeling. I did K for years in high school. We would drive around on K listening to Lil' Kim's "Hardcore" and not understand how we weren't friends with her. K is a disassociate drug, and it's actually pretty fun. Although, it's cat tranquilizer and a total '90s designer drug, so it's not very cool to get into K now. It comes in a liquid bottle for a lot of money, and you have to bake it or blow-dry it until it turns into a powdery form, and then you sniff it. It's like the feeling you get when you focus your eyes on something but can't really see it—like when you zone out for a minute. Well, K is like that for a few hours. Your eyes get all blank, and everything is kinda quiet and weird, and you look really fucking creepy to other people who aren't on it.

Crystal meth is a whole other ball of wax. It just occurred to me that I spend a lot of words at the end of the book warning girls about heroin but I'm all whatevs about meth. There's a reason why it's so popular these days. It's pretty good. I'm not gonna say that it makes you feel "totally free" or "really motivated," you can hear that on True Life MTV specials or whatever. All I can say about crystal meth is that it made me wanna dance for hours, fuck for hours, drive for hours, smoke for hours, and then, eventually, cry for hours. Coming down is worse than you can imagine. Like a bad acid trip meets chemo meets watching your parents die in a car crash. Fortunately during those days crystal was a real West Coast thing and it was hard to find, hence my lack of warnings about it. I'm sure if I were raised in LA instead of New York the back of this book would be all about how dangerous meth is.

To be honest, it makes me sick to describe drugs. The thought of describing ecstasy just made me throw up a little bit in my mouth. What I'll tell you is that I never got in trouble for doing drugs after that first time I smoked weed in junior high. If you really want to know what drugs are like, you should do them for yourself. And if you want to know what happens when you do them too much, you should keep reading. I called my old friend Lydia. She's a teacher now. (Why are all my old friends teachers? I guess that's the only job our generation gets offered.) I asked her about the day we started doing a lot of drugs.

Lesley: So what about the day we started doing drugs?
Lydia: Yeah! We drove to Connecticut for a rave, from Boston. And I remember very clearly what the place looked like inside, all these white walls. It looked like a really big apartment. That was a fun weekend. You flew up there and you almost missed your flight on the way home, you did miss the flight and you had to go on a later flight. And you had to call your dad.
Oh yeah!
Yeah. And then like on Sunday, you had to go home. We raced from that dinner which was far and you missed your plane. But it's just like the shuttle flight. They have them every hour but we were so upset, we thought you were going to be in so much trouble. And then they put you on the next one like it was no big deal.
That was the first rave I ever went to and I had never done any drugs. I had smoked pot, a little bit maybe, and drank.

And then I did ecstasy and it was like . . .

Did I tell you to do it? Did I suggest that was a good thing for you to do? [*Laughs*]

Well no, it was like, the whole plan of the weekend was that you were like, "You have to meet my friend Susan, we're gonna go to a rave." I think I probably asked you, "Do you do ecstasy or whatever?" And you were like, "yeah." I showed interest in wanting to do it. And then Susan said, "I'll get the pills I'll get everything, don't worry about it." At the time, I was still kind of a hardcore kid but we were young and it was just a lot of dudes and I remember not fitting in. I think I was just over punk and I wanted to find out more about stuff going on in the world. So raves were the next step. How many people in the rave scene were disgruntled punks who got sick of where it was going huh? Probably most. When we went I remember this feeling—it was just techno music and I was just standing there, like, "This is it? This is retarded."

Is that a question? That's probably the longest question in this whole book.

Sorry, I've had way too much coffee today. Then Susan gave me a pill [*Both laugh*] and an hour later . . . a medley of Frenching people [*Laughs*] and sweating and standing out in the rain and being like, "I've arrived" [*Both laugh*], and then . . . I did crystal meth.

Do you remember Heidi Gobbo was there?

That petite girl from Huntington.

You two had like the same hair cut and you were both the same size. And I remember Susan said, "We gotta keep them under control," 'cause you . . . [*Laughs*] Do you remember taking your shirt off? Yeah. I swear the two of you had like . . . [*Both laugh*] . . . were dancing with your shirts off. And remember the whole time, Susan kept saying, "You gotta take care of your friends!" So I had to take care of the two of you and then I had Jane, who was moping around like a big Pooh Bear that night, because everybody was kissing and Jane had never kissed anyone, boy, girl.

Wow, what a square.

Yeah, so she had this whole emotional breakdown about how she had never kissed anyone and she wanted to kiss someone. So I got to be the lucky first one and then you go, "Lydia, you don't want to kiss me?" And you were mad at me and then we kissed.

DYKE! Instead of *psych*! Yeah we all sat in a circle and took turns kissing each other. I can still see you walking me around trying to walk it off but Susan gave me crystal meth that night and I remember exactly how that felt. Nothing ever felt the same as that ever again. But the first time you do something like that it's just so *much*.

Is that a question too?

FEBRUARY 1996 · 11TH GRADE-AGE 16

DEAR DIARY,

Today I smoked with Larry and Michelle and I was FUCKING BUGGING. I swear, I never want to smoke weed again. I was soooo thirsty and they kept eating these really salty chips with no water or anything and it was driving me crazy. They seemed like they weren't high but I was so fucking high, so I felt weird that maybe it was affecting me more than them and they knew it. I cut the rest of the day and went home and watched *The Breakfast Club* with the blanket over my head.

UPDATE · Weed takes a few smokes before it works. This wasn't the first time I smoked weed, but it was the first time I really got high. Hoe lee sheet. You know that high. The high that changes all highs. The high that makes you start to question drugs. This is the worst high. What starts as a soft voice in the back of your head, something like, "Maybe my teachers are right about drugs being dangerous," suddenly turns into Sam Kinison shouting through a megaphone: "NOBODY LIKES YOU," he screams, or "YOU'RE DOING IT WRONG YOU IDIOT!!!!" The panic of smoking weed "wrong" starts to set in, and everyone around you is eating chips realllllly slowly, and there's no water around, and you're wondering how they can be eating chips with no water because you're so fucking thirsty and maybe there's something wrong with you because you are thirstier than they are. Maybe you smoked pot wrong! You don't know what you're doing! You will never, ever, ever be cool! Go home!

I hated pot so much after that and would continue to do it until I got it right. How else are you supposed to make friends in high school? Pot unites the hippies, the jocks, the thugs, and the metalheads. It was the only thing that brought all those little cliques together, and because I had always hung out with older kids from the hardcore scene, I needed to work the weed angle, which wasn't so much an angle as it was a circle (of love). (JK.)

FEBRUARY 1996 · 11TH GRADE-AGE 16

DEAR DIARY,
I went to visit my sister at Syracuse last weekend. It actually was really fun.

UPDATE · The weekend I went to visit my sister at her college was the first time I tried cocaine. She and her friends got some and then they went to get beer, and they left me alone in the dorm and told me to keep an eye on the coke. I was wearing clips in my hair and got bored, so I took the clip off my head and dipped it into the bag just a tiny bit and sniffed. My throat got slightly numb, but that was it really, I hadn't done enough to get any kind of high. Or maybe I did get a little high but wasn't able to recognize the subtlety of good coke. When she and her friends got back I gave them the coke, safe and sound. I didn't tell my sister, but I told her best friend, Ricky, what I had done. Ricky laughed and was like, "You rule."

Lesley: When was the first time you ever did coke, Leigh?
Leigh: I think I did it maybe once in high school. It was not something I ever did back then. It's actually not something I did until after college.
I did a lot of coke senior year. Were you at my house the night . . .

Yeah when we were doing the combo? That's the only time I really remember.

"CK1." That girl Andrea was there and we were making her do K.

Yeah we thought it was really funny. We were like shoving it up her nose.

Haha.

Yeah we were like, "She thinks she can handle coke. Wait until this." How mean is that?

Oh man, it's so fucked up. We were like, "Do it! Do it!" It was horrible. But it actually was really fun. Doing coke and K together is a good high. It's starting to occur to me that I wasn't this innocent victim of bullies who managed to overcome hardships and was, in fact, a self-centered and evil bitch who liked to fuck with people and then conveniently forget it. Oopsies.

FEBRUARY 1996 · 11TH GRADE-AGE 16

DEAR DIARY,

Last night was Thriller and I got really bad E, puked, the whole nine. Very scary. I don't want to make myself upset, I don't want to be an emotional wreck. I slept all day today. The only thing I'm worried about is Mr. Casey because I cut 7th period but he saw me in the hallway. My bag got stolen, so did Lydia's and Emily's. When it comes down to it, life is so pointless. Is there anything cooler than punk and rave? I hope so. I'm starting to hate everything again but I really don't want to! Why am I finding it so hard to like anything? The only thing I like is staying home and going out.

UPDATE • "The only thing I like is staying home and going out." You know who else likes that? Earth.

Punk was for misfits, and rave was a place to do drugs and dance. Both are bullshit. The real "scene" is based on hanging out with people because you like them and not giving a shit about a scene. As soon as it becomes a "thing," it's over.

MARCH 1996 • 11TH GRADE-AGE 17

DEAR DIARY,

Tonight we got sold out of the Helium show so Emily, Judi, and me went out cruising the city. We blasted Deee-Lite and were all happy, first time in a really long time. I had a great time just driving around. I think I understand Lydia a little bit more, Emily a little bit more, and myself a lot more.

UPDATE • The night we couldn't get into the Helium show and blasted Deee-Lite in the car instead is one of my favorite memories. At every traffic light we got out of the car and started dancing. In the book *The Perks of Being a Wallflower* the main character talks about the feeling of being infinite and those moments that are so small and so perfect and can almost seem to sum up being young in one night, or one song, or whatever it is that makes you feel untouchable for that one moment. That was one of those times that I truly felt in the moment, like everything would be OK one day.

DEAR DIARY,

I find it so amusing how I'm able to remember such words as Mescaline, Thorazine, LSD-25, Quaalude, etc. and tell you what each of those things do, yet I simply cannot remember the periodic table of elements or this week's vocab words. Emily told me she wanted to try heroin. Of course I don't want anything horrible to happen to her but I feel like in some ways I do. I know that's a bad thing to think. Sort of like, "Haha I was right, I told you you'd get addicted to coke and heroin, you hypocrite, you fool, you waste . . ." I love her but she has driven me so crazy this year. Another thing is that my dad just told me that his business was failing. I kind of feel like I knew that all along. It feels so sad to see your father fail at something. You can try your whole life at doing something you believe in but sometimes you just fail. It's your fate. It's just so sad to me because he's my father you know?

UPDATE • When I read these entries all I can think about is how much time I wasted being miserable. I think the real story with adolescence is the lows are way lower and the highs are way higher. When you're feeling ugly you are a hideous troll, and when you have a good night you lie in bed buzzing for hours and hours. Fun fact: Feelings pass. Ever feel really angry? Try eating a sandwich. Chances are, the feeling of anger will pass because you're just having an LBS (low blood sugar) moment. Another fun fact: Boredom isn't a feeling. Boredom is an excuse for feeling something else and not wanting to deal with it. My problem was that I was so me-based. I was always looking for something more, something outside of myself to fill the emptiness I felt inside. You know what else is me-based? THIS BOOK! Anyway, don't worry. I start doing heroin soon.

If you're so bored, start a project or something. Make art or do a zine or get a part-time job and use the money to make a giant Polaroid collage of all your friends.

MAY 1996 · 11TH GRADE-AGE 17

DEAR DIARY,
I've been thinking a lot about Lydia and all the fights we've been having. We have been drifting apart ever

since she decided to get married. I wrote her a letter saying how important it is for us to stay friends but it really isn't. When I am with her, I always have the feeling that I'm supposed to apologize for something. I always feel like I am guilty of something but I haven't done anything! I don't want to hate her but I guess I do. I actually think I might hate her a lot. I just want to show Lydia, show everyone that I'm not stupid and I'm not nothing. Someday I will write a book that will make people cry and laugh and tie knots in their stomach and change their lives.

UPDATE · How awesome would it be if, as you were reading this entry, you realized you had dried tears on your face from a previous entry and that made you laugh and then you looked down and couldn't help but notice your stomach was in a knot and you were like, "My life just changed"?

Lesley: Why did we stop being friends?
Lydia: The short answer is I was jealous. I thought you had more opportunities than me. Your home was always so comfortable and your mom was always so bright and interesting. You had good things that I didn't have and I felt like you didn't appreciate them.
Correct.
Also I *haaated* Darlene and Charlene. I really thought they were bad. I thought they weren't smart. I knew that they did a lot of drugs.
So that's why girls stop being friends. They eventually real-

ize the other one is spoiled, or one of them wrecks the friendship by bringing in other people.

Darlene hated me, and you started hanging out with Darlene. **Did she?**

She would never make eye contact with me; she would never talk to me. She was like ugh, still to this day, I shiver at the thought of Darlene because she was the snobby girl in 7th grade, you know, who no one really knew what she was thinking but everyone just assumed you were on her bad list because she would never crack a smile in your direction?

Darlene was probably jealous too. Young girls are so territorial about friends and boys and scenes. They can be really vicious. I don't know this for sure but I get the feeling guys are just, "Oh, Eric doesn't like me anymore? Okay, I'll hang out with Rick."

It's just sad. You know, I was looking back through the hardcore pictures. And there's like no girls and the girls that were there, I was looking at this one picture and it was all these guys and me and Loretta and I'm like, "How did I hang out there? Like Loretta and I wouldn't talk, we had nothing in common." Whatever girls were around, they just couldn't support each other.

I hate girls who hate girls. Where's all the Ya Ya Sisterhood of the Traveling Pants kind of girls? I was never a part of a girl friendship that didn't have that drama and jealousy.

Well, whatever drama or whatever we went through together made us who we are. Maybe we had to have all that evil stuff go through us so we could see what it does to relationships.

I later asked Darlene if she hated Lydia:
Lesley: Lydia said you hated her. Did you?
Darlene: I remember this one time she came up to me at a show and said, "You make me sad." And I was like, "Why?" She said it was because I didn't always say hi to her or something.
Gay.

LOSING
MY
VIRGINITY

✳

MAY 1996 · 11TH GRADE-AGE 17

DEAR DIARY,
Last night was a super night! Me and Pavel were a
little flirty. It was worth waiting all week for.

UPDATE · The next million entries are about my relationship with Matt Pavel, who became my first real boyfriend
after a lot of pushing, pulling, mix tapes, and boring, redun-
dant diary entries. Matt was a totally cute sXe kid who loved
Japanimation, *Star Wars*, and the Smiths. He wore baggy
hardcore-kid clothes but prepped it up a bit with argyle
sweater vests and button-down shirts that I frequently borrowed. He had brown hair and a high tolerance for all the
shit he put up with, considering I was just starting to get into
drugs and he was straightedge. Ironically, today he drinks
and I am straightedge. I've put together a shortened list of
greatest hits from these pages to describe my Matt Pavel year.

JULY 1996 · SUMMER-AGE 17

DEAR DIARY,
Today Matt Pavel called me. At first I didn't know it was him.

JULY 1996 · SUMMER-AGE 17

DEAR DIARY,
I just really think Matt Pavel is MSALM (My Secret Agent Lover Man).

AUGUST 1996 · SUMMER-AGE 17

DEAR DIARY,
Tonight I gave Matt Pavel *Less Than Zero* to read and also the lyrics to an Archers of Loaf song. I hope he loves both things.

AUGUST 1996 · SUMMER-AGE 17

DEAR DIARY,
I fucking kissed Matt Pavel last night and now I rule this entire planet!!!

JANUARY 1997 · 12TH GRADE-AGE 17

DEAR DIARY,
I had sex with Matt last night.

UPDATE · Matt was my first for most of the majors; I lost my virginity both orally (on him) and vaginally with him for the first time. I believe I lost both on the same night.

Him going down on me came a few weeks after that, but Marisa was really the first.

I didn't like sex the first time; I didn't even like it the first 10 times. For starters, it really hurt. I remember I placed a towel underneath my half-naked body because when I read Judy Blume's *Forever*, that's what the main character did—you know, for the blood. There wasn't very much blood, but I did feel like I was being torn apart. I just didn't understand how his penis was supposed to fit inside me, let alone feel good. Let alone feel amazing! The whole world loves sex. The whole world talks and thinks and writes about it constantly. Even my friends at school had assured me that it was the best thing ever. "Sure, it may hurt the first time, but after that it gets better." But it didn't get better that quickly, and I assumed for a long time that there was something wrong with me. When other girls masturbated, did they stick dildos up their vaginas to simulate an erect penis? I didn't. Had I been doing it wrong all these years? Even when I later had sex with my junior-high-school crush, Andy McDaris, whom I was so hot in the pants for, it still didn't feel good. I remember the tears forming at the corners of my eyes as I told myself over and over in my head, "Please don't cry. Please don't cry." The only thing worse than having painful sex, I thought, was crying over painful sex. Today it is not like that. My body changed, my hormones, and, for lack of a less douchey term, what turns me on and what does not. Today I understand how "that thing" is able to fit inside me, and today I understand (sometimes) how it can even feel good and how it can feel amazing and even how it can feel just "meh." My recommendation to younger girls who are having sex for the first few times: Get drunk. Sorry, mom, but it helps. I don't mean to say that in order to do it you should be wasted and get taken advantage of. What I mean is that for most girls, it fucking hurts, and if you want to do it and you honestly think you are ready, then you could do with a little social lubrication. Oh yeah, regular lubrication can sometimes help too, so try that approach before you try Jäger shots. Sorry if that sounds a little *Girls Gone Wild*, but whatever. Getting drunk helped my sex life. I'm just being honest.

Another thing that is highly suggested is wearing a condom. If you think wearing a condom is lame, then please read the book *Random Family* by Adrian Nicole LeBlanc. The reason why there are no abortion entries in this book is because painful sex or not, I always made sure to use a condom. If it sounds like a dumb '90s Rock the Vote type thing, then good. Plus when you do start enjoying sex, you can be sure that a condom will make the whole experience last a lot longer.

What's weird is when you are blowing a guy and you look at his face. His eyes get all sleepy and his mouth hangs open and he looks like a cross between an infant taking a nap and Terry Schiavo. You don't need beers for a BJ, just a Zen approach going into it so you don't laugh out loud while his dick is in your mouth and you choke on the damn thing. Being eaten out is your time to shine, but the sad truth is that most guys don't know what they're doing. In fact, the dudes who usually claim they are so good at giving head are usually the worst at it. If you are a guy and you're reading this, I recommend looking up "The *Vice* Guide to Eating Pussy."

I'm not just trying to plug *Vice* here. I actually gave the article to my boyfriend in college and it shaved four months off our breakup.

FEBRUARY 1997 · 12TH GRADE-AGE 17

DEAR DIARY,
I cheated on Matt with Curtis and I can't stop writing it down. He is so adorable. I want to be at his house right now but he hasn't called me and I don't want to beep him because then I'll be sweating him. Oh man. I'm sorry Matt.

UPDATE · Matt Pavel and I went out for most of my senior year of high school. Not the best year to start a committed relationship. Everyone knows senior year is about partying and cutting class and hooking up in secret with the guy your best friend has a crush on. Senior year is not for cuddling. Around March, I cheated on Matt for the first time with this kid Curtis, who was skinny and dorky and used to steal his dad's medication.

BTW when you cheat on someone, never write it down. You will ALWAYS get busted. I know that's like Cheating 101, but for some reason in my life I've acted as though I were above the law and have always written it down and HAVE ALWAYS GOTTEN CAUGHT! BUMMER! Curtis was so cute from afar. He was thin and pasty and wore glasses and had short hair. He wore gray T-shirts and jeans and had pretty blue eyes and long eyelashes like a girl but in truth I think he often felt very self-conch-shell about the way he looked. I guess that's the reason he started taking steroids. Poor guy, he could've been my real-life Harry Potter.

FEBRUARY 97 · 12TH GRADE-AGE 17

DEAR DIARY,

I want to write more about Curtis right now. I want to replay everything that happened. We were at his house, chilling, smoking. I took a muscle relaxer and that combined with the one-hitter made me feel pretty nice. He pulls out his bed and we're both chilling on it. Every now and then a phone call or a change of position. He touches my knee with his knee. Hmmm. I decide I want to talk about the shit he and his ex-girl did but I don't think he's quite down. He offers me gum and we keep moving closer. Our feet are touching and rubbing together just a little. He touches my arm to get a piece of lint off. Then I start playing with the buttons on his shirt. I touch his face and it's really soft. And then we kiss. We kiss and kiss and kiss and then I get a page from my mom telling me to come home. 15 minutes I tell her and then I get back on the bed and get on top of him, legs spread apart. We kiss kiss kiss. He puts his hands up my shirt and I'm not wearing a bra. He tried to go down my pants but I tell him no. We dry-fuck and it feels really good. I can't wait to kiss him again. We spoke today in school and everything is cool. He's so stupid but so adorable. I just want to fuck his brains out.

UPDATE · Isn't making out in someone's teenage bedroom just about the hottest thing you can think of? Curtis had a total boy-next-door vibe. I tried to find Curtis for this, but it just wasn't happening.

FEBRUARY 1997 · 12TH GRADE-AGE 17

DEAR DIARY,

I have to write a 4-page short story but I can't. I've never written anything longer than two pages. I've been thinking about K maybe a little too much. I know it's bad, I know I know. This is so unlike me. I don't even want to think about that word— ADDICTED. Yuck. I want Darlene to call me. I just beeped her. It really sucks that she hates Charlene; I wish they would just make up. The only reason why I hang with Leigh and the Bitch Crew lately is to get fucked up. Fuck. I love writing that word. Fuck fuck fuck fuck fuck. I hate this time of year, February. It's nothing. It's sandwiched in the middle making my skin look pale and my clothes worn out. Too early for prom, for spring. I don't want to rent movies with Matt and I don't want to drive around looking for weed spots. I want to talk to Darlene. Call me call me call me save me from my bedroom and home-work and boys and drugs. Now.

UPDATE • The fight between Darlene and Charlene was legendary in the scene. What happened was Darlene and Andre got Chinese food and went over to Charlene's house to eat it. They were eating it in the kitchen when Charlene's dad walked in and said, "How can you bring food to someone's house without having enough to share?" Or something like that, and Darlene I guess was really embarrassed (although she wouldn't admit that at the time), and she and Andre left and thereby claimed to never speak to Charlene again because Charlene didn't stand up for them. Even though I didn't say it, I kind of thought Darlene was overreacting. I don't think my dad would care about food, but if he did, I wouldn't argue with him. I'd be too scared, and I bet Charlene was too. This past winter Charlene got released from a 3-year rehab and she, Darlene, and I all hung out together. It was actually real-ly fun, we all got along, and Charlene was doing really well. Now I believe she is back on the junk.

MARCH 1997 · 12TH GRADE-AGE 18

DEAR DIARY,

People Think I Am	I Really Am
Obnoxious	Obnoxious
A good listener	Charming
Independent	Impatient
A bitch	Paranoid
A weirdo	Sensitive
Confused	Emotional
Annoying	Independent
A sweetheart	Serious
Serious	Indifferent
Political	Shy
Loud	Can't talk to adults
Dorky	Bratty
Corny	Dorky
Stupid	Flirty
Irresistible (Ezra)	Smart
Cheap	Cheap
	Creative
	Lazy

UPDATE · Me me me me. Only a teenager could sit and write out 34 adjectives describing herself. Who cares what people think about you? As Winston Churchill said, "What people say about me behind my back is none of my business."

MARCH 1997 · 12TH GRADE-AGE 18

DEAR DIARY,

I've been thinking a lot about Bahamas and prom and I'm not really that excited. Bahamas is two days away and I just picture me struggling, uncomfortable, competing . . . How can I rise above this stupid shit? I used to be able to. I'm planning on doing a lot of drugs. That is my escape. I'm going to the prom with Ezra, which I am sort of not looking forward to, only because when other people are around he goes into dick mode. After the prom is the Hamptons but I'd rather go to a party with Darlene. I'd like to be able to write poems all the time. It usually ends up being boring journal entries such as this. To some people, this is another language and they wouldn't be able to read it. Right now I have a bottle and some crystal, so all I need for the trip is a phat pill and I'm all set. I really love drugs. Is that sad? It just helps me think with a different part of my brain and right now I just don't want to stop writing so I'm gonna write about drugs.

Crystal: It keeps me awake and up up and happy. I need to stay awake but I won't take too much. I can't crash. It reminds me of Meltdown with Susan and Lydia. What a strange night. I felt my feet moving without my brain, I felt it warm up my heart and my ribs. Lydia told me my eyes were so big and I was so sweaty but I couldn't feel it. The crystal was called

Pink Champagne and at one point I went outside and it was pouring rain and we all danced around in it because it was the most beautiful thing we had ever felt. All the scary strangers became my friend.

Special K: The first time I did it, it didn't work. Maybe a very little. I met a cute boy who I'll never see again. I do K and I'm in a bubble. Things become circular. K reminds me more of school days, when I got fucked up in health class and couldn't speak and I feel like Mr. Fritz totally knew and I was so upset but there was nothing I could do. We put our desks in a circle and then I became the circle within the circle and then I went to the bathroom and never came back. K is me and Darlene and the moon with a rainbow halo. It's thinking we were all friends with Lil' Kim. Thoughts just spin off my head and become round at the edge. I like it but I feel like it might burn my brain.

Ecstasy: Holy shit. The most intense out of all of them. So many stories. Sticky lollipop hands. Sweaty, dirty, nasty, smelly, retched. E stamps, no inhibitions at all. White tank top, no makeup, dancing so hard I can't even remember my feet not moving. I was a blur. Blue and Whites with Michelle at Vinyl. We were so in love with the music, each other, the snow outside. It was freezing and we were so dirty and we fell asleep in the subway station but we were still happy. We walked to Ezra's house in the snow with our arms around each other. Now it's different, it feels different. In DC the Christmas lights became little bugs. I can't even tell if it feels good anymore.

Acid: It's hard. A tightly wound-up feeling, my body and mind become a tightly wound-up ball of string that slowly starts to unravel. In the beginning there are smiles and giggles but nothing is really that funny. Paranoia was extreme but then there were pretty patterns in the sky. It turned plaid. The yellow Ryder truck, the bathroom stall, the stains on the walls looked like dinosaurs. My mind was supreme suddenly and I became so secure and so fucking cool. I promised never to do ecstasy again after I look around the room at dozens of ravers with lollipops. I start giving them out; the ravers were BEGGING for lollipops it was so gross. I spot kids in a corner sucking in from a gas mask. I see Sam Adamson and I feel inferior. I want her to be tripping too but I don't know how to communicate that. An ugly boy keeps touching me. I saw pebble imprints on my palms, they remind me of fossils. I say hey guys, look: fossils. No one else could see them.

Marijuana: Is all paranoia and cottonmouth. It is hyper for me. It reminds me of Emily and a gravity bong, Larry's house, kind bud, bad trip. Go home out of breath and fall asleep. I stole my dad's bowl and packed it with Leigh at the commons to watch the skater boys. It tastes like shit, I pretend to be high. I hate weed. It's about Leigh, Kate, my parents but not me. Many laughs though. Sometimes I like it.

Drinking: In Lydia's backyard with Emily and sober Anita Fower. Lydia tells me about the girls she's loved. We take off our clothes and I throw up in the toilet. Very late at night, Lydia screams at RT. Everything was about RT, not us. Food Express, a cemetery, a parking lot, a lot of beer. Zima with Leigh at the Clubhouse. Whatever.

Cocaine: Is dancing fast and being awake and restless and bored and smoking smoking smoking and talking so much about nothing at all. The more I think about it, the more I want to do it. I don't know why.

Right now I want to get fucked up. I want to smoke dust. Angel dust, dips. I know it's gross but whatever. The K and the crystal are at home. I would do it if I had it.

UPDATE · I felt a little wary going to the Bahamas because I was going with this whole crew that wasn't really my crew and I didn't know them that well. In high school I didn't really have a crew, which didn't seem important until senior year. So I got in with Leigh's thugged-out crew, whom I liked, but going on vacation is a pretty intimate experience. It ended up being awesome, one of the best weeks of my life. Though maybe that's just the ghost of crystal meth speaking. I carried it on the plane in my underwear.

I was in high school, senior year. I was 18. I loved drugs; we all loved drugs. We all did drugs, and the gross factor, the scary factor, the sad and pathetic factor—those were all fun factors. When you're 18 the world of danger and excitement only happens in books like *On the Road* or in fun drug movies. That is where excitement exists, certainly not in the everyday life of a teenage girl. We drove around fucked up, thanked God we didn't die, and then did it all over again. When you grow up in the suburbs, the horror stories exist only in passing. They become things that only happen to someone a friend of a friend knew but they were never about us. In a way I think we were so bored that we were almost challenging the universe in that sense, egging on consequences because we were starving for something to happen. I know I was waiting for life itself to teach me a lesson. It never really did.

APRIL 1997 · 12TH GRADE-AGE 18

DEAR DIARY,

I just spoke to this woman on the beach who is a Rastafarian. She's from London, then Baltimore, and now Nassau, Bahamas. She said she went to raves. She basically spoke to me like a Jehovah's Witness, which kinda freaked me out. I mean, I don't believe in hell but it's probably because I don't want to. Maybe it's the devil's trick—to make people not believe. We spoke about the year 2000 and how something is definitely going to go down. She said that the world was going to explode spiritually. I told her I liked doing K and E but she said that because they are synthetic I should never do them, or else . . . and I thought she was going to say I might overdose but instead she said, "Or else you will go to hell." Then I started thinking about what if I do go to hell? I guess it's pretty bad and according to her I am going to hell because I'm not repenting for my sins or whatever. She asked why I'm not doing that and I said, "I'm just not into planning for the future." It's true that I believe in living in the Now and doing what I need to do to grow spiritually. If that's a sin then I guess I will go to hell. I'm sure it won't be so bad considering I'll know a lot of the people down there.

UPDATE · This Bahamas trip and Rastafarian situation happened after I got accepted into college. My deal was this: I got my tongue pierced around the same time I applied early to Bennington. I got rejected from Bennington and never showed my family my tongue ring. It was easy to hide. I didn't talk to them that much. After I cried over Bennington, I applied to Bard, Hampshire, Sarah Lawrence, and some safety school like SUNY Purchase or something, I don't remember. I got rejected from Bard, wait-listed at Sarah Lawrence, and accepted to Hampshire. I wrote my essay about my experience in kick line (that's like cheerleading but all dance moves, no cheers) being a feminist statement, and

Hampshire fell for it because that's how they roll. If I had included a tampon they would have given me a scholarship, especially if I were a black Native American with AIDS. I was so sick of colleges at that point that any acceptance was fine with me, so the day I got the letter from Hampshire I told my mom I had good news and bad news. The good news was that I got into college; the bad news? I stuck out my tongue and showed her the glistening silver ball. She was so happy I got into college that she didn't even care about the tongue ring. A year later I realized that having a silver ball pierced into my tongue was pretty stupid, and I took it out. Then I got my nose pierced, but the stud fell out in my sleep, and the hole closed up.

Turned out everyone had a piercing at Hampshire, so you ended up looking like a real rebel without one.

JUNE 1997 · 12TH GRADE-AGE 18

DEAR DIARY,

I hooked up with Squid!! (Oh My God.) I also bugged out on Matt. Fucking Darlene told Matt about Andy and Curtis and how much drugs I've been doing so now Matt is totally over me and has no love. I don't think he gives a shit about me. I can and I can't live with that. I bought a gram of coke off Shady. I don't know why, I never bought coke before really but he was hitting on me and I didn't really have anything to say to him. I really don't have any clue as to what the fuck I'm doing. Just having fun I guess. As long as I continue to keep writing everything will be OK. Being a slut and a drug addict–JAP, jock boys, rapists . . . everything I used to be so against is becoming my life. Maybe it's because I never really knew what I believed in the first place. I believe in: Bikini Kill, Bobby, writing, *Party Girl*, having fun, experience, Jen from Gogglebox zine (which I can't find but if I had it, I'd read it every day), looking good, Sam Adamson, all books.

UPDATE • It was a shocker that I hooked up with Squid because he was the goof of the group. Everyone has them. He's like a spazzy, crazy guy who will eat a spider or make himself puke if you ask him. I was so boy crazy I hooked up with the court jester. Such was the case with Squid for about two months. We did a lot of cocaine together and got into fights. It was all very surreal. I guess we called him Squid because he was a squirmy little fucker. He couldn't sit still for like 5 seconds. I hadn't spoken to Squid in about 10 years, and I wanted to see what happened to him, what he was like. Even though we had a psychotic sort of relationship, I always felt like under those layers of crazy he was a sensitive person who really had low self-esteem because he was kind of short and annoying and everyone called him Squid, which is not an attractive nickname. Man, do I love those underdogs.

JULY 1997 • SUMMER-AGE 18

DEAR DIARY,
Squid is playing me like WHAT and I can't stop writing things down. All he wants from me is a blow job

or sex. Doesn't he notice me kissing his ears, his cheeks, his eyelids, softly, slowly . . . ? He is quick and fast and rough just like Andy who doesn't even talk to me anymore. I don't even think about Matt. Ever. I hope he doesn't think about me.

UPDATE · Matt did think about me. He even made a zine about me—how I was evil, how much I hurt him, etc. That's what emo dudes do. They hate women and listen to Sunny Day Real Estate. Poor things. Squid and I tried to do it a few times, but it only ever really happened once, in the car. We even got a motel room once, but we didn't know what we were doing. Just because I had done it before didn't mean I was able to just jump right into it again. I was not good at having sex until the end of my first year of college, and that was because I had turned into a full-blown alcoholic. I wanted to like sex; I wanted to do it a lot. Neither thing worked out for a while.

Lesley: Squid? Hey, it's Lesley.
Squid: What's up Lesley?
How are you?
Good how are you sweetheart, how's everything? How you been?
I've been awesome. Everything's really good.
No doubt. So what, I hear you're writing a fucking book or some shit?
Yeah I've been working on this book. It's about stuff I used to write in my diary . . . and I wrote a lot about you.

What the fuck you writing about me for? You can't write about me. You can't write on paper about me.

Well, I wrote good things about you.

OK, as long as it's good things.

So what have you been doing for the last 10 years? (Immediatly after I say this I realize that it's the worst question ever.)

I don't know. I went through it. I went through a lot of shit, I'm sure you went through a lot of shit. Hell yeah.

Do you want to tell me about going to jail?

What do you wanna know about going to jail?

What did you go away for?

For drugs.

Are you sober now?

Yeah I'm sober.

Are you in any kind of recovery program?

Recovery program? Oh hells no!

Well, I just called to say hi and see how you were doing. I wanted to let you know that I wrote about you. I liked you but I guess we were both really fucked up.

Yeah I know. I was definitely really fucked up then too, but I appreciate it. You know that.

AUGUST 1997 · SUMMER-AGE 18

DEAR DIARY,

Tried to fuck Squid tonight but it hurt like a bitch. The backseat of a car is not the right place for that. I think I kinda really might like him, which is bad bad bad because he is mean and immature and I probably can't make him what I really want him to be. I want to be in shotgun in his car all the time. I said, "Squid do you still have a crush on me?" And he said, "Yes." And I said, "Are you sure?" And he said, "Yes, do you think I'm lying?" Sometimes I do and sometimes I don't!

UPDATE · He was one boy in a very long line whom I was interested in changing, making them what I wanted them to be, what I thought would work for me or what I was entitled to have. Just because you are a whiny teenage girl looking for love doesn't mean you are supposed to get it. This is where every teen movie and book has it wrong. Teenage boys don't fall in love with the poor, sad girl who waits by the phone and opens up to them about how much they hate their dad. For years I figured that because I had waited and longed for the perfect romance that I was entitled to get it. I thought I knew what I wanted, and I truly believed that if I was strong enough, I could change a guy and make him who I wanted him to be, but not even Hulk Hogan can bend minds. I think for some people, they never come to this realization and go through life either hating their husbands, divorcing, or being too scared to get involved in the first place. It is something I still struggle with to this day. Control is tricky. I feel like once I have surrendered to the fact that I'm incapable of turning a man into the kind of dude that I want, he eventually becomes the dude I want!

AUGUST 1997 · SUMMER-AGE 18

DEAR DIARY,

I'm high outta my skull right now and it's 4 AM and Squid dropped me off to do something shady with Shady so I'm at home tweaking and about to get fucking restless. No one is out, my mom's awake, my car is blocked in and I have work at 12 PM. I beeped Squid but I doubt he'll call back, I beeped Beth but she's shady and probably not doing anything good. Fuck!!! I want to be out right now!! I'M AWAKE AND ALL I WANT IS FOR SOMEONE TO CALL ME BACK SO I CAN HAVE A GOOD NORMAL CONVERSATION WITH THEM!! I WISH EVERY-ONE WAS WIDE AWAKE AND TWEAKING AND FREAKING OUT LIKE I AM RIGHT NOW!!!

UPDATE · Coked up in your bedroom while your parents are just waking up and your car is blocked in and you have work in a few hours is a place I think no human being would ever like to revisit. I did a lot of cocaine that summer. It took me to places I would never dream of going to, like Flushing, Queens, at 6 AM or Long Island nightclubs where I wore black pants, tight black shirts, Toast of New York lipstick, and Red Jeans perfume. Just remember that doing coke can be fun, but for every amazing high you have, you are going to have the shittiest, most insanely horrible com-ing-down process ever. I have literally contemplated jump-ing out of windows when I was coming down off coke, and I'm not talking about doing baby bumps off a key in the bathroom of a party, I'm talking about doing line after line after line after line and smoking and smoking and smoking and sucking Jolly Ranchers or giving BJ's just to keep your mouth moving.

COLLEGE

AGE 18–22

GETTING
COOLER

✶

SEPTEMBER 1997 • 1ST YEAR-AGE 18

DEAR DIARY,

I'm in Hampshire now. Just started college. Away from everything old. It's so sad and strange and exciting. I met two jungle heads today who seemed to like each other a lot more than they liked me but that's OK I guess. I'll give it time. I'm just not into talking talking talking about myself and the things I'm interested in all the time. I just want to party, laugh hard, and have a fucking fun time. I need a party crew or at least an amazing awesome friend. I met this girl Mave. She's beautiful and smart and talkative and I guess just too nice. I keep meeting all these "nice" people and it makes me feel really cynical. I feel like I have to walk on eggshells because everyone is just so FRIENDLY, so fucking nice, it gets BORING. What's your name where you from what's your dorm orientation group what do u wanna study????? Blah blah

blah. Ezra I wish you were here, you'd be making fun of everyone with me. I haven't used my crack sack once. Please let me find some crackheads!

UPDATE · "Crackheads" was just an expression we used at the time for people who were into drugs. Remember your first week of college, when you cling on to people who dress the same as you? For me it was reallllllly baggy jeans and Polo shirts buttoned all the way up. Little did I know that look defined the "electronica" crowd.

When your friendships are based less on personality and more on who's punk or who's a raver or who's in a band, you end up with some pretty incompatible friends. Like Mave. I "broke up" with her about a week after meeting her because we had nothing in common (PS Ezra was my prom date, remember?).

Meeting boyfriends and having sex is one thing, but going to a new school or a new town (or both, as is usually the case) and making new friends is really hard. You have to court them just like a lover, and then when you realize you have nothing in common with the person, you have to undo all your courting to get rid of them. That's usually the hardest part. I don't know how guys do it without coming across as gay. It must be hard. Anyway, all these Big Pant Little Shirt people wanted to talk about was music, and that can get really fucking boring, especially if the music you are talking about is drum and bass. "Oh yeah, I totally love the part in that song when they go brweidwax liwnedfiwex ws xiwneid. Then it slows down and gets all spacey. That track's more intelligent drum and bass than jungle." I also realized that I really only liked that kind of music when I was fucked up. And these new friends weren't into K and crystal meth. Unfortunately.

OCTOBER 1997 · 1ST YEAR-AGE 18

DEAR DIARY,
I miss listening to the Smiths in Matt's room. I miss watching *Party of Five* with him, going to see *I Know What You Did Last Summer*. "To die by your side, what a heavenly way to die." "There is a light that never goes out." I miss him drawing my name in graffiti. I miss him driving my car. I miss playing him my new favorite song and making it become his new favorite song too. I miss Christmas time and this time last year. We started holding hands in public. Yesterday would have been 1 year and 2 months.

UPDATE · I started missing Matt (guy I lost my V to) when I had no one else. I guess you don't know what you got 'til it's just you surrounded by a bunch of dumb college freshmen listening to socially conscious wigger music and talking about "bombing the suburbs." I did not end my relationship with Matt on good terms. I tried breaking up with him a bunch of times, only to have him beg and plead, "We can work on this" style. I still see him around sometimes, and we are cool with each other but not really 100% cool. It wasn't like it was some romantic relationship. I was 17 and he was 23. WTF?

OCTOBER 1997 · 1ST YEAR-AGE 18

DEAR DIARY,

Right now my body is 1 mescaline, 2 Tylenol, 1 NyQuil, and a whippet. Head throbbing. Hands shaking. My parents are coming at noon. Headache. It's thinking about it that's making it worse. I should just stick to my regulars. Fuck E, fuck acid, fuck mescaline, fuck pot, fuck shrooms. These are supposed to be the "all good" drugs. All the "healing" and "experience" drugs. Yeah, it's an experience. A bad one. So stupid. All they ever made me realize was how stupid either I was or everyone else is, when I know already. I need sleepy time now.

Hearing rainfall

Outside onto the concrete

Sounds like little electric lights

Popping on my hair and in my ears

(I wrote that while I was tripping last night. Wow it's so deep.)

UPDATE · That was the first night I did mescaline and also the last. It didn't do anything except give me a really bad headache. It was probably fake or something. I did the mesc at "Hampshire Halloween" AKA "Trip or Treat" AKA the biggest party at my school. It was rumored to have been listed in *Playboy*'s top-ten college parties once upon a time, and we had all heard stories about how one year a guy was tripping superhard, took off his clothes, and rubbed feces all over himself and told people his costume was "a piece of shit."

Hampshire seemed to support and encourage drug use during Trip or Treat. It was never said out loud, but they provided a bouncy castle and free water in the "chill-out tent." Everyone knows that bouncy castles are for getting your E to kick in superfast. It's not like anyone at Hampshire College was 8 years old.

DECEMBER 1997 · 1ST YEAR-AGE 18

DEAR DIARY,

It's 6:45 AM and I am TWEAKING! Doing lines on my bed Laura Palmer style. Cocaine is evil. All I want is more. It's scary. It's horrible. I only have a little left. I don't know what to do. I was at Robbie Addams' house all night. It was kind of fun but not really, just weird. He went down on me and kissed me but I couldn't even feel it, it was like nothing. Coke does not make me horny like everyone else. I gave him a BJ just so he would leave me alone. I feel myself coming down and it hurts.

7:15 AM. I don't want to write. I don't want to do anything. But I have to do something. This is so fucking horrible and scary. All I can think about is more and more and more coke and I've already done so much. I wish I were back at Robbie's house doing lines. What do I do now? I don't want to be a cokehead but I feel myself becoming more and more addicted. Every health class was right. Every teenager was wrong. What do I do now? I don't want to do anything but more cocaine! I hate myself right now.

I hate school. I don't want to go back tomorrow. Oops, I mean today. Fuck. Nothing is right for me. I am so afraid.

UPDATE • Robbie Addams gave me the best cocaine I've ever done. I started to wonder what happened to him, and then a friend told me he killed his fucking parents! I didn't believe it, but someone sent me the link: "A Long Island man admitted in court today that he killed his parents—a husband-and-wife legal team—last fall, then set fire to their upstate vacation home to cover his tracks." Apparently he did it with a butter knife and admitted it, but his family still stood by him, claiming drugs made him do it. He got 25 years.

My first instinct is that it's a cop-out to blame drugs. It reminds me of all that *Reefer Madness* hysteria, but coke benders can take you to a really dark place.

Now, maybe he was just unhappy and used coke to stay happy, or maybe those horrible comedowns are what made him an unhappy guy. What came first, the chicken or the cokehead?

I feel disgusted and ashamed and regretful and weirded out that I hung out with a murderer . . . It's pointless to think that. I didn't judge him then and I don't judge him now.

I should focus on the harm drugs brought him, but part of me can't forget how great the coke was and how much fun we had. I can still see him cutting up lines on this huge piece of poster board he had that said "I Scored a Goal at Robbie's Bar Mitzvah" in big gold, glittery letters.

FEBRUARY 1998 · 1ST YEAR-AGE 18

DEAR DIARY,

Erin Gibson died. I always thought she'd be the girl to live forever. The poor little rich girl. A huge wedding. Red roses. Divorce maybe at age 30. Really nice car. That was Erin. Trashy rich girl. The pretty bedroom with the huge bed and mosquito netting thing that I always wanted. She shaved her armpits too early, I remember those red scars. Girl who was able to get any boy. She said she'd beat up all the mean girls for me in 7th grade. We almost got beaten up at Adventure Land because of her. I can't believe it. She's dead.

UPDATE · We went to Adventure Land, and even though we were tweens and it was the early '90s we somehow stumbled into a scene from *The Warriors*. We were just middle-class kids who wanted to go on rides and eat candy! Suddenly all these guidettes stood around Erin in a circle, their long purple nails glistening in the hot sun. They had acne scars like cherry pits, crop tops, and crunchy hair that didn't move. They circled around us and kept asking Erin, "Do you have a tissue? Can I borrow a tissue?" We didn't realize that was mean-girl code for "You must stuff your bra." Erin just ignored them, but I could tell she was scared. We were all scared, and for years every time we passed Madonna Heights, the school for bad girls, I imagined those girls trying to set off cherry bombs in the principal's office.

We promptly left Adventure Land, hearing Erin's mom

bicker all the way home about how she had just dropped us off and what was the problem? No one would tell her that our beloved fun park had become *Land of the Lost.* I'll never forget sitting in the backseat with Leigh, trying not to sing along to "What's Up?" by 4 Non Blondes because it was corny. Erin turned the radio up and said, "I love this song."

She died in a drunk-driving accident our first year of college. She was one of the girls from 7th grade who had basically saved my life. She went to the other middle school and had my back. Her toughness, real or imagined, in turn made me feel tough and invincible. Kind of like the way boys feel after they watch an action movie.

MARCH 1998 · 1ST YEAR-AGE 19

DEAR DIARY,
I can't stand to look at myself in the mirror. I don't want to wake up in the morning. I feel stupid and ugly. I'm the ugliest person ever. When does it stop? When do I get to wake up feeling pretty? Why am I so concerned? Why is it so important to me? My professor Michael Lesy says college is just a series of identity crises. It's so true. Every day I write the book. Sigh.

UPDATE · A constant theme that runs throughout all these entries is insecurity. No matter what, I was never "something" enough. I was never smart enough or pretty enough. I just wanted so much, and when I didn't have it I tortured myself. I either avoided mirrors or spent an enormous amount of time in front of them, constantly checking myself out in windows on the street. Sometimes I would go to the bathroom in the middle of class just to make sure I looked OK. Extreme insecurity and extreme narcissism are about one pube away from each other. There are like 6,525,170,264 people in the world. Who was I to think I was anything-est? It makes me feel so sad that I tortured myself with all that nonsense.

APRIL 1998 · 1ST YEAR-AGE 19

DEAR DIARY,
Last night I did dope with Charlene. I'd say it was equivalent to taking about 8 NyQuil. I puked, I itched. It was like dopey pills of E. I was sweating nuts. Then I chilled and enjoyed it but it wasn't like *Trainspotting* or the most intense orgasm or anything like that. I passed out in Charlene's bed as if I had been drinking all night. She did more than me and drove around, ate ice cream and cheesecake. Insane. I was in puke city. I still feel nauseous. I never want to do it again. It's possibly one of the dumbest things I've ever done anyway. All I want to do right now is puke all of this shit out of me. Hopefully tonight I will be able to drink.

UPDATE · That was the first time I did heroin. Charlene, the girl who was BFF with Darlene, who had never even liked drinking or smoking pot, but then fell in love with a guy who was a junkie. Next thing I know, she is one too. The guy didn't like her before the dope, and he didn't like her after. She ended up moving upstate after her parents cut her off, and we didn't hear from her for years. One day she was having a major stomachache and thought it was a case of really bad diarrhea. She went to the hospital and the doctor said, "You're 7 months pregnant and you're in labor." She gave birth to a little biracial boy and signed his rights over to her parents. She then went to rehab, and there she stayed for 3 years. You can't go to rehab for 3 years and expect to come out and be normal. Recently I saw Charlene at Darlene's birthday party, which was awesome, but when I went to say good-bye she was locked in the bathroom and wouldn't open up.

Lesley: Were you doing dope the other night at Darlene's party?
Charlene: No.
When I went to say good-bye to you, you wouldn't come out of the bathroom. You were in there forever. Why?
Because I was doing a little bit of coke.
I don't understand how you can do coke without dope.
I don't know. You can. Coke is just fun sometimes.
Anyway, do you care if I use your name or tell the story about when you gave birth to Elliot?
No.
You're sure?
Yeah I mean it's a pretty good story.
It's a great story. So what are you doing today?
Trying to get gas money so I can drive to work. I'm sorry, I'm really out of it right now.

Ok, I'll call you later.

OK. Bye.

[*I called Charlene back and her phone had been shut off.*]

I don't know why I became a junkie. When I did it that first time years ago, Charlene and I drove around in her red BMW convertible. She happily ate her cheesecake while I was dying. That is heroin. Afterward she told me she needed to stop by someone's house to pick something up. "Wait in the car I'll be right back."

3 hours later she came back. I didn't mind so much because I was in a cloudy heroin haze. After the puking I felt sort of drifty and it was easy to sit still for 3 hours. It had taken her so long because she actually went over to this dude's house to have sex with him. I was so fucked up I couldn't even get mad. Then we had a sleepover, but she tried to spoon me, and that was weird because we had never snuggled like that before. I drove home early the next morning and vowed never to do heroin again. I was glad I had tried it because now I knew the truth.

As I type this I can feel my gag reflex twitching like an invisible baby's finger is twiggling it.

JULY 1998 · SUMMER-AGE 19

DEAR DIARY,

Darlene is now a Jehovah's Witness and it was soooo weird talking to her tonight because when she tells me about it, everything seems to make sense. She kept talking and talking and talking about it and I felt myself believing her. It's like when someone talks a lot about something you don't know about, you start to agree with them just because you can't argue with them. It's completely insane! She's giving away pictures; she gave me her amazing glittery prom dress because she said it was too sexy and her really cool Breakbeat Science T-shirt. The one that says DRUM AND BASS FOR A FUCKED UP PLACE because she doesn't curse anymore! She's in a cult, I get the hand-me-downs. Not bad.

UPDATE • Darlene gets in a Chinese take-out argument with Charlene, so one becomes a junkie and the other a Jehovah's Witness. WTF?

Lesley: Hi there.
Darlene: Hi!
So let's cut right to the chase. I wanted to ask you about becoming a Jehovah's Witness. I wrote a lot about you and Charlene, and Charlene went one way and started doing heroin and you went the total opposite way. Do you feel like your parents fucked you up and that in turn made you do drugs and then turn to JW, or did it not have anything to do with them?
I think it had to do with my real dad abandoning me. I was just over a year old when my mom and me left him and it didn't make sense to me until this year when I met a kid who is, like, three months old. I looked at him and I realized that he knew who his parents were. Until that I didn't think I

remembered being with my dad, but I did. I used to have a really bad pattern with boys where I would get them and then I would rip them open. I was horrible to them and that had to do with my dad, I think.

Well what's the short version of how you got involved with Jehovah?

I guess I was always interested in other people's religions because I wasn't raised with any religion.

Is that why you did drugs too? To maybe seek out a deeper meaning . . . ?

I think I did drugs because I wanted to feel high. I don't think I was trying to escape anything.

OK.

So the JW thing was that I met this guy right after I was at this hippie commune thing. I was really open to anything. I was studying Shamanism, Buddhism, whatever. I came home and worked at this dumb job and this guy started talking in a way that was . . . enlightening, I guess. Nobody else was talking like that so I gravitated toward him. I was open and I was like, "I'll give this a try but either I'm gonna do this 100% or I'm not gonna do it at all." So I just did it 100%. For eight years.

What happened in the 8th year?

Well, it wasn't really the 8th year. I had gotten married to him and I didn't like him. I thought that he could help me become this better person that I never thought I was. That was the reason why I married him. That's not a good reason to marry someone and eventually I just couldn't be with him anymore. I was becoming almost suicidal. Then everything started to bother me about the people . . . most JW's were really closed.

How do you mean?

They were like, "Being homosexual is the worst thing you could be," and meanwhile the Bible didn't even say that. There were chunks of people who weren't like that in JW, and that was the part I was attracted to. There were some who were nonjudgmental and loving and I took from that experience. That part was really good. When I decided to leave my husband, I was ready to leave the whole JW scene. It wasn't alive to me anymore, it became about "You can't do this, and you can't do that . . ." People were creating more rules than there really were. They were like, "Don't ever let your kid play extracurricular sports because they'll start associating with worldly kids."

It was a cult.

Yeah! It wasn't even biblical. There were some who were like, "OK, everyone calm down," but they were outnumbered. So I was just like, "I gotta get out of here."

Do you still read the Bible?

No.

Do you still believe in God?

I think so. You know what happened? I chose to leave, and with that decision I was like, "If Armageddon is real I'm just gonna die in Armageddon." It was a choice I made, I either live now the way I want to and die in Armageddon or I live really uncomfortably and maybe, if it's true, survive Armageddon.

So you think there will be Armageddon?

I think if it happened I would not be surprised. You know?

Like, World War III?

No, like serious Armageddon. Like, the Creator is gonna evaporate the earth or freakin' . . . destroy the bad people. It's destroying the people who didn't want to live by God's rules.

So do you still believe in those rules?

I think I consciously blocked it out because if I start thinking about it I'll get really guilty.

Well, you can try to see the Bible as a metaphor, I guess. Like "Armageddon" is a metaphor for maybe, like, the death of love.

I guess.

A lot of people study the Bible as a metaphor, not literally.

OK.

I don't know, maybe it would make you feel better if you didn't take it literally but used it as a metaphor, like, to do good. I don't read the Bible so I don't know; I'm just throwing around ideas here.

It's just not something I want to revisit because I've never been this happy in my life. I've figured out through a lot of therapy and thinking too hard that the way I've been acting my whole entire life is a reflection of some series of traumas, and it totally makes sense. I've learned how to maneuver through life in a nonchaotic way. Now I'm in a relationship that is the closest I've ever gotten to another human. I guess I was just afraid of everything the first 27 years of my life, and now I'm kind of breaking free. I'm really happy.

And you train dogs?

Yeah, and I love it. And I have one thing to add to that—I

can't tell you what to put in your book or anything but one of the reasons why I'm successful as a trainer is because I have applied therapy to working with dogs. I teach dogs to not be afraid of what they're usually afraid of.

Oh, like the dog whisperer. Do you watch that?

Yeah, of course. But I think I'm in it for a different reason, because I feel like I'm opening another person up when I open a dog up.

So it's like the same stuff you used to do to guys, but now you do it to dogs and it's more positive?

Exactly. Totally.

Sounds good.

Another thing I want to tell you before we end this is that you can say whatever you want about me, good or bad. I'm giving you permission to say anything bad. I own everything that's happened in my life and I'm not ashamed of it. So you can say anything at all.

Noted.

SEPTEMBER 1998 · 2ND YEAR AT COLLEGE-AGE 19

DEAR DIARY,

I'm at Hampshire again, in Prescott Mod 100, which is awesome. Everyone talks here, no one listens. The only person who ever really listens is my mom but today she said, "Why don't you take some business classes?" When she makes comments like that I want to hit her. I just want to go to every rest stop in America. I want to hang my clothes on a clothesline and wear yellow rubber gloves when I do the dishes.

I want to be a librarian; I want to marry a janitor. I want to smoke crack on the highway. I want to go to a prom. I want to eat cheese doodles in the car and wear a black hoodie sweatshirt. I want my car to break down at night. You and I will run into a haunted house and kiss for hours. I want to drink whiskey and watch a movie somewhere far away. I want to see the weather change when I drive. I always want to hear your voice in my house, I love that sound. I wish we were brother and sister trapped in an attic. I wish we were driving to Nebraska, we could make out in cornfields. I want to lick your arms that are all strong and sweaty because you have been digging and farming all day. I'll make you oatmeal and then we'll drive and drive. I want to go fishing and not talk for hours.

UPDATE · After I couldn't find a real boyfriend, I fell in love with my diary, and even though it doesn't have a penis, it was a real man. Outside of this relationship most of my time was devoted to hanging out in my on-campus apartment (Prescott Mod 100—Mod stands for "modular apartments"), being a fag hag, doing whippets with my gay friends, drinking Pabst Blue Ribbon, taking bong hits, not having sex, and putting on 20 pounds.

APRIL 1999 · 2ND YEAR-AGE 20

DEAR DIARY,
I know Brian does not have "those" feelings for me, yet at the same time I cannot help but think that

every time I see him there is some kind of chemistry. He curls up on the couch and his hair is all messy and I just want to eat him up. He must know that I think these things. At the same time, our friendship is increasing at a rapid rate. We talk a lot and I feel as though I can trust him. Yes I want to kiss him and touch his body and curl up in the folds of his arms when we are on the couch alone at night. His head is so close and you know I just want to touch his hair and kiss his ear. He is extremely funny and he can teach me a lot while at the same time I would like to teach him a thing or two, about talking and becoming close and feeling comfortable with yourself, that sort of stuff. A while ago I didn't think our friendship would go very far but now I feel like I will miss him when he's gone. And I will write him letters and not let him forget about me too easily. His birthday is soon and I would like to get him *The Secret History*. Even though he doesn't want to kiss me, I still look forward to speaking to him and seeing him every day and it's not just on *Twin Peaks* Tuesdays, it is every day. The sad thing is that I don't even care about hooking up with anyone else. And I doubt I even will. Being Brian's BF for the rest of the semester is fulfilling enough I think. I'm sure I'm asking for a little blue balls but you take what you can get. In this case, I'm getting more than usual.

UPDATE · Hampshire was small and incestuous. There are no grades there either. Seriously, I got, like, a "dolphin" in math. Every professor just wrote written evaluations based on our work. There were no tests either, just papers and projects. The purpose of this kind of education is to free students from the pressures of being constantly rated and use the freedom to really let their creativity blossom, but to us all it meant was, "TIME TO FUCKING PARTY!"

Most of the students were antisocial and awkward, which was cute and charming for about 5 minutes. For me and my friends, if you were quiet and weird but semicute (5's were passable for having sex; remember, it was college, there were only 1,700 students, and we were wasted), we either made out with you or ignored you. A favorite pastime was playing Spin The Bottle, just as an excuse to have a sexual interaction. I made out with all my friends, we were that bored. I mean horny. Having sex with someone at that point was pretty much just great gossip. I did it with a few people that year but only when I was really drunk. OK, maybe not a few. Just two.

Since Brian and I were such good friends, I made out with someone else. His modmate Lance at a party. Lance was cute and fun, and I'd always assumed he was gay-ish. Thinking someone might be gay was not enough to stop me from hooking up with them. Sometimes it could even be more of a reason to. Lance slipped his arms under mine and around my waist, and I was stoked. Finally someone to take my mind off Brian, you know? Armed with my 2-liter bottle of Coke spiked with Jack Daniels, I ran off into the night with Lance, where we swapped spit under the stars and continued to drink enough so that we'd have something to blame it on. Everyone knows the only way to get over a crush is to start liking someone else. I thought Brian would be relieved. Oddly he wasn't.

APRIL 12, 1999

DEAR DIARY,

So Jesse and me took some Valium and smoked some weed and then we bought lots of shitty food and ate it and watched *NewsRadio*. It was fun. When I went food shopping with Brian yesterday I finally told him that I made out with Lance. He responded in a really weird way. Like I think it bummed him out. Maybe just because they live together. I don't know. It seemed like he was kind of mad at me.

UPDATE · Lance was a dork. He was totally that dude who always wore Hawaiian shirts, but he ended up giving me great head one night but I hear fags sometimes love eating pussy, so who knows. Today he lives in LA with wife and baby. I envision him working in "pictures." I wasn't into Lance, but I had to show Brian that he liked me, so I fooled around with Lance. This is a very sink-or-swim method that's exactly like when you have a cold and you drink whiskey. Either you wake up the next day and the cold is zapped, or you are now REALLY sick and with a hangover to boot.

Of course, it annoyed me somewhat that it took me making out with Lance for Brian to realize that he liked me. I pushed those ugly feelings aside and promptly started sleeping with Brian. We had a big romantic (well, as romantic as you can get in college) convo that ended with a French kiss and me leaving and then him calling me and walking back. It was all very drunk and dramatic and wonderful. We proceeded to date each other for the rest of the year. Mostly it was all about *Twin Peaks* marathons, drinking, fooling around, memorizing the words to "Nothin' but a G Thing," and him having explain to me how important it was for him to finish his thesis on Kierkegaard.

APRIL 1999 · 2ND YEAR-AGE 20

DEAR DIARY,

I slept at Brian's last night. I am in awe. I am incredibly happy, as well as exhausted and confused. Overwhelmed with emotions. What the fuck is going on? This whole thing is not going to end well I know that. I asked Brian if the only reason he likes me was because I was hooking up with Lance and he said no no no no no but I don't see how it can be any other way.

MAY 1999 · 2ND YEAR-AGE 20

DEAR DIARY,

Sex with Brian was fun. That was 2 nights ago. He's away right now and I'm feeling a bit Lloyd Dobler and it scares me. What if I skipped NYC and ran away with him? Nope, would never happen. Nor would I want it to. It's just that sometimes he can be so Lloyd Dobler too (and sometimes Diane Court). Regardless, the end of the semester always brings this. Things are perfect and then they end. Am I supposed to make monumental movements or just go with the flow? We'll see. The semester's not over yet.

UPDATE · I really liked Brian, which was why I was constantly watching the movie *Say Anything* and making comparisons to it. There are probably another two dozen entries about the guy.

It was his last semester, he was graduating, and I was only at the end of my 2nd year, but I was totally geeked out. He was the one who started it, the one who wanted to get involved with me when we were just gonna be friends. When we became more than friends it got awesome, with cute little notes left under doors, mix tapes, hikes to the top of a hill after we'd sniffed a bunch of Ritalin, talking about college things like *Star Wars* and *Family Ties*. We had sex in the middle of a wheat field. We threw a TV set off a building just to hear the amazing pop it makes when it hits the ground and then proceeded to "neck like two Puerto Ricans playing hooky." He actually went down on me in the stairwell of the library, where it was filthy (literally—there was dirt and twigs and old piece of gum all over the floor), but it was superfun to brag about to my friends the next day.

Then school ended, and for him it was forever. For me there was just a summer of promising to write letters and maybe even a visit. I was happy for him to start his new life, sad for me to realize I wouldn't be a part of it.

Apparently Brian didn't give me the benefit of the doubt and maybe thought I was way more in love with him than I really was? He came for a visit while I was staying at my sister's apartment in Manhattan and he was with friends in Brooklyn. It was raining out and he slept over, and we watched movies and made out and talked about music and life and things that might happen and things that might not.

The next day we made plans to possibly go dancing that evening. I walked him to the L train and gave him a kiss on the cheek. That was the last time I ever saw or spoke to Brian DeGary.

For months I tried to think what I had done wrong. Did I smell bad? Had I said something deeply offensive? I went to my parents' house in Long Island and kicked rocks for weeks. I didn't want to talk to my friends and tell them what had happened. "You mean you still haven't heard from him? Did you try calling his friends in Brooklyn? Maybe something happened . . ."

What happened was that he was just a huge fucking pussy. After a little while I got over it, and that was that. Brian lives in Santa Fe now with his girlfriend and no kids.

Brian: Hello?

Lesley: Hi is this Brian? It's Lesley Arfin.

Lesley Arfin, what's going on?

The reason I'm calling is because I'm writing a book called "DEAR DIARY . . ."

Yeah I've totally seen your column before.

Well it's essentially the same thing but I'm interviewing the

people I wrote about. And incidentally I wrote a lot about you in my diary.

[*Silence*]

Um, I don't know if that shocks you but um . . . we were really good friends for a while and then we were seeing each other. And I think the last time I saw you, you were getting on the subway. Do you remember that?

Yes, I totally remember that. I remember it so well. It's funny because I remember that exact moment. I remember we were talking and, like, the next time we were gonna go do something, we were gonna go visit your parents in New Jersey?

No. My parents lived in Long Island. I thought we were supposed to go '80s dancing. Visiting my parents is hardcore! I wouldn't blame you for not talking to me if that was the case. No, we were supposed to go '80s dancing and then I never saw you again and for a long time I just felt like I had done something wrong. Did I smell bad or say something offensive?

No! Not at all. It's so funny. From my perspective, what I remember is just being so fucked up in my head at that point. I had just graduated from college. I just remember feeling so messed up.

Well, I think I was pretty self-centered then and couldn't really understand what it felt like for you to graduate. I was just too crushed out.

This is actually something I've thought about a fair amount. The thing is, we were such good friends. I remember we used to have so much fun together. I always thought you were the coolest, greatest, most fun person to be with and hang out with. And so why did I do that? I don't know. I guess I just became a total fucker. I feel horrible that I made you think that it was something you had done. That was absolutely not the case. It was just me . . . freaking out.

Well, that happens. But you could have called me!

Yeah, it would have been a simple thing to do.

I feel like when we went from friends to making out, it meant a lot more to me. And I knew that but didn't care.

Hmm.

I knew you were graduating. I'm sure I put some pressure on you. But let's see, I walked you to the subway station. We said good-bye and you got on the train. Where did you go then?

God I don't remember where I went that day. But you know what else is sort of interesting, now that I'm thinking about it, is that I was so insecure at that point! I think conversations that I could see myself having in a relationship was so "whatever," I just wasn't able to have them. Like very honest conversations. Any conversation that was like, "Where is this going?" I just wasn't able to do that back then.

That's funny because you seemed so mature to me. For so long I had so many things I wanted to say to you. I always fantasized about running into you and what I would say. I created these scenarios in my head until one day, it just didn't matter anymore.

Well, I'm really glad you called me. This is something that I had definitely regretted for a long time. I never knew how to make it right. I felt like if I had gotten in touch with you, I just wouldn't know what to say. I guess I just thought you would tell me I was a dick. I'm so happy to hear from you now.

Yeah I don't know you anymore but I'm sure you're not that different now, so maybe you're an awesome dude. When I never saw you again and made my peace with it I just thought, "Well, I guess he's just a pussy."

It's probably true in many ways. It's probably a very fitting description.

SEPTEMBER 1999 · 3RD YEAR AT COLLEGE-AGE 20

DEAR DIARY,

Fucking Hampshire. I'm back here now. It smells like school. I am SO hung over. I never get this hung over. Last night I was terribly drunk, passed out way too early. Passed out on Jesse's floor. Jesse's being weird, I feel like he doesn't like me or something. Austin smoked all of my cigarettes. It is raining and I have no friends. Jesse is only happy and nice when he's fucked up and Austin is only happy when Jesse is happy. This semester is going to be so odd. Maybe I should go abroad. I am so hung over. I saw 2nd-year Kevin tonight and I think he's cute. I'd bone him.

UPDATE · Kevin was skinny and zitty and wore pleated pants from the Gap that his mother bought for him. He wore white T-shirts from Kmart and a green windbreaker and New Balance sneakers, and he wore this every single day. He also had a pair of gray fleece pants, which he described as his "Saturday Pants." And then he had a pair of pajama pants, and he called those his "House Pants," which ultimately became his nickname. He had bright blue eyes that looked like the bottomless Crescent Lake when he was high and short brown hair that he would sometimes shave all off. He loved fast cars, drugs, loud music, chess, and Quake. That was it. I don't think he ever loved me, but I sure loved him. We would get high and smoke and I would put on a Rolling Stones album and he didn't even know what it was.

Kevin is a year younger than me, and after he graduated from Hampshire he moved to LA and continued to do heroin, as well as a tremendous amount of crack. He even came to visit me at rehab totally high. It got so bad that he traded his car—which was an Audi—for, like, 4 bags of heroin. Eventually he came clean to his parents and went to rehab.

He called me from rehab and we talked and when he got out, he went back home to New York and took me out on his parents' boat. He kind of peer-pressured me to go body boarding, but we had a nice visit and promised we'd talk soon.

Then he relapsed. Then he got clean again. I was crazy about him, and I miss him a lot because today he refuses to talk to me (except to say he wants absolutely nothing to do with this book, "in any way shape or form"). But in short, he was my entire 3rd year at Hampshire. When I first met him, it was the closest I have ever come to feeling love at first sight. Everything he didn't know, every cool band and cool reference that just boggled his mind, well, that just made me love him more. He won chess tournaments and majored in math. He was the coolest person I had ever met, and then one day, everything changed.

SEPTEMBER 1999 · 3RD YEAR-AGE 20

DEAR DIARY,

It's 4 AM and I can't believe I'm still awake. Austin is an amazing person. Just amazing. We had the best conversation right now. Talked about girls and boys and Jesse and family and pop culture and sarcasm and wit. I miss Jesse. Thinking about him makes me sad. I hate him so much right now. I'm glad he's leaving tomorrow. I really want to cry when I talk about him. I left a note under his door. I don't care if it makes me vulnerable. That's a bullshit game and he's a real friend. I won't be bothered with pride.

UPDATE · Jesse ended up being the editor of *Vice* and quitting junk soon after. Today he is basically my boss. He and Austin remained best pals until Austin started dating Jesse's ex-girlfriend. Now Jesse hates him, and Austin doesn't speak to any of us.

DRUGGIE

OCTOBER 1999 · 3RD YEAR-AGE 20

DEAR DIARY,

Last night we were all bored and didn't feel like getting coke because it's such a mission and $$$ and it was Sunday so we couldn't go to the liquor store. I was like, "Let's find some heroin," kind of as a joke but Jesse and Austin were like, "Yeah!" But we didn't know where to get it and then Sasha came out of her room and she goes, "Did you guys say you wanted heroin? Because I sell it." And we were freaking out because it was THE FIRST THING SHE HAS EVER SAID! HA HA HA AMAZING! She didn't have any though but she said she would get some next time.

UPDATE · I was excited by the idea of doing heroin again, not because I liked it so much when I did it the first time when it felt like I had taken a bunch of NyQuil, but because it seemed cool. I'd be lying if I said it was for any other reason. I was bored, restless, and aching for experience. Because I hadn't gotten addicted the first time, I assumed the second time wouldn't be any different. I didn't want to be scared of anything, especially something that would make me feel good. Something that would make me feel incredibly cool.

I've heard heroin being described over and over again, and with few exceptions, like Hubert Selby Jr., most never really nail it. If they did, maybe more people would be less curious to try it. For me it wasn't like "ten thousand orgasms." It's like the very few seconds after the orgasm. The gentle tide that drifts you out to sea and carries you off to sleep. It hits you hard and lasts for hours. It's the tide that hits you in the ocean of Sunday-morning back scratches. Try to imagine how it would feel to be a melting candle or a poured drink. Imagine if you were a sweater and the boy you liked wore you all day long. I know I'm still not getting it right. On heroin,

the endorphins are hip to hanging out for a while. It's like the minute after you come lasting for hours. And the gentle wave doesn't carry you off to sleep but just lets you linger on the warm sand for as long as you please. Eventually you have to wake up and go to class. Eventually you have to find that high again. You will. People say no high compares to your first high, but that's a half-truth. The first high is the best only because you have nothing else to compare it to. Every other high after that gets compared to the first but it's really not an issue. Junkies become junkies because heroin is really good. It works. It makes you feel free and warm and beautiful—all the things it promises. The campaigns are correct. Junkies may not look hot, but they think they are. If heroin was about the chase, junkies would just stick to being cokeheads. And some do. And that's why there are tons of crackheads. Personally I never was into the chase.

The first time I shot up was a few weeks after we sniffed it. Kevin was slightly scared and hesitant, but I wasn't. I was of the school where if you are going to do something, do it right. I still belong to that school. The difference between shooting heroin and sniffing it is like the difference between smoking a joint or sniffing it off a pin. And smoking dope is just a waste, that's like Drug Addicts 101.

When your life changes—and I'm talking about major changes: a death, a birth, a sweet sixteen, a graduation—it's not really a monumental experience. It just sort of happens. and deep down inside it's like you always knew it was going to happen that way, so it doesn't really feel important. When we started to do heroin, that's how it felt. It was like I had found the thing I was always looking for. It just made sense, and that was that. There was no freaking out on my part, no major guilt. I knew it was wrong, bad, addictive, dangerous, but so was everything else I did. I didn't think that this was much different. I didn't really write in my diary for the next year. The whole time was dedicated to copping, lying, stealing, fighting, loving each other more than we actually did, and just overall partying (it was pretty fun. I only write in my diary when bad shit is going down). There are a few entries, but for the most part I was afraid to write down what I was doing. If it was in print, it meant that it was true. This is one of the entries:

JANUARY 2000 · 3RD YEAR-AGE 20

DEAR DIARY,

Last night Kevin and I couldn't sleep. My knee hit the wall and when I woke up there was blood all over my leg. I didn't think I had kicked the wall that hard and I can't believe if I did kick it that hard, it didn't wake me up. We both have the flu it sucks. I can't sleep.

UPDATE · We didn't have the flu, we were withdrawing from heroin. Kevin came over and told me that he thought it wasn't the flu, that we were kicking, and I was like "Oh yeah! You're right. Cool!" and we were all, "This is it? It's not that bad. God people whine about this and it's really not that bad." And once we realized that's all it was, kicking dope, we did some more.

I feel bad about glorifying heroin. It's killed so many people

I know, and it's been associated with *Vice* for so long, what with Suroosh starting the magazine after rehab and everything. They've lost about a dozen friends and contributors since that magazine began. The thing about it is, yes, it does feel really good. Like a nice sleepy-time hug from a million friendly babies that love you. However, it's also a gun pointed at your head every time you do it. Is this stuff purer than what you're used to? OK you're dead. Or maybe you get a bit drunk and do too much because you're not paying attention. Dead. Or maybe you mix in some pills because they're around. You don't think you're going to do anything that stupid obviously, but when you're shitfaced, shit happens. Dead. How about if you quit and move on and you're celebrating some new stage in your life and someone has smack so you figure, "Why not?" because you're drunk and you think you finally conquered it. Dead. Actually, that's how most people seem to die from it. They quit, move on, their tolerance goes down, and then what looks like a tiny line is actually a lethal dose because your body's no longer used to it. Dead. There's also the slow and painful way to die from it, and I'm not talking about something obvious like AIDS. Sharing needles gives you hep C, and that can lead to liver damage and then liver cancer and all kinds of other things. When you're a junkie these diseases just sound like a bunch a pans clanging together, but when you actually have them, you don't just have a little vacation in a hospital and get better. You DIE. It doesn't matter how much money you have either, it all comes down to a fucking slow, very painful death. So when you hear about an ex-junkie dying of liver cancer, don't think he just had some real bad luck and you never know what the big guy upstairs has planned for you. Dead. Or what about the ex-junkie who hanged himself? He was just depressed, right? And that was why he did heroin? No, the hep was eating him up inside, and he knew it was only going to get worse, and doing the heroin just warped all his endorphins and made him sadder and sadder every day so he ended it all. Dead. So the junkies you see OD'ing before your very eyes are only a small fraction of the ones who die from it.

I had one experience with this dude Leon who used to keep jars of piss in his room. He OD'ed on me. He had been drinking a bunch of beers and then sniffed a bunch of dope. After five minutes we realized his lips were blue, and so the four of us (three girls and one boy) lifted all 190 pounds of Leon and cleverly put him in the shower. This was a smart idea—and by "smart" I mean "dumb"—because now not only were his lips still blue, but his 190 pounds of dead weight was now soaking wet. So what, add like 10 more pounds to that? Sasha was against bringing him to the hospital, but what other choice did we have? We were just a bunch of spoiled brats who at the end of the day had no idea what the fuck we were doing. We never pretended to be hard. We never pretended to be broke, or be anything other than what we were. And that night when the shit hit the fan, we were fucking clueless. Each one of us struggled with a dangling limb heavy as a sandbag. When we finally got Leon down the stairs, his head hitting every step on the way down mind you, he was soaking wet, maybe dead, and it was 20 degrees outside. We pushed him into the car, and suddenly he opened his eyes. "Where are we going?" He asked. But he was alive. He was alive!

"And why am I all wet?"

I felt happy and joyous and free and did a little dance around the car, punched Leon in the arm a couple of times for old times' sake. Then I got my dope and left. Kevin and I broke out immediately. Had we already had the dope before the whole incident, I highly doubt we would've helped revive Leon.

NO FUN

JUNE 2000 · SUMMER-AGE 21

DEAR DIARY,

I met this boy, Darren, through all the old UMass kids I used to be friends with. He's friends with Jeremy Willis. Really cute, kind of a pussy. I wanted to go home with his roommate but I went home with Darren. I picked the wrong one. I had a dream last night that there were little girls all around me singing songs from "Annie." Darren said I laughed in my sleep. I'm pretty sure the rest of the dream was about death though.

UPDATE · Darren was a hapless, cute, nice guy I ate up and spit out. He briefly played in an electroclash band, and that was his fleeting period of utter coolness. The rest of our time was spent doing heroin, playing guitar and singing songs, talking about sci-fi books and comics, and . . . that's it. On heroin you never really sleep. It's a constant state of being in between asleep and awake. So I would lay in bed and drift, aware that my bedside light was still on but too asleep to turn it off. In that lucid state I would have horrible nightmares. While physically I felt like I was marshmallow over a campfire, mentally I was the campfire, thrashing around in the fiery pits of hell. It wasn't pleasant, so I would just sniff a few more lines to keep Satan down and try to melt back into the space between the chocolate and the graham cracker.

JUNE 2000 · SUMMER-AGE 21

DEAR DIARY,

I guess I am crushed out on Darren a tiny bit but is it in the dope or the drink, or is it in my gut? I can forget about his roommate, especially when Darren is buying me flowers and kissing me in the rain. I can't help but constantly be thinking about fucking his roommate though. He's so hot. Darren is just so passive. We'll see, no commitments necessary. Darren is very pretty. I mean, he's just beautiful. Maybe even too pretty for me.

UPDATE · This relationship was doomed from the start. All the heroin did was drag it out. That's yet another downside with that drug. It makes you so complacent you could be with the worst person on earth and you'd be all right with living with them forever. You could live with Courtney Love and 16 orphans in Oakland in the winter with hemorrhoids and nothing on TV but endless episodes of *Mad About You* and you'd be all, "I could get used to this."

JUNE 2000 · SUMMER-AGE 21

DEAR DIARY,

Great night. Besides the reading and all my friends being there and going to Gavin's house, etc., the rest of the night went like this: Me and Darren got in our underwear and did dope all night, listening to the Neutral Milk Hotel. We stayed up all night long, asking each other stupid questions and falling all over each other all fucking night. I can't believe what a night we had! This morning he took a shower and I slept and he made me iced coffee and we walked to work together. I like him.

UPDATE · Gavin is the other *Vice* guy besides Shane and Suroosh. These were the good days of heroin. The honeymoon. At the time I convinced myself that I was a casual user, the first of a thousand lies. That summer the evenings were breezy and warm. I would lay around in my underwear and feel beautiful. Leaning out the window on Avenue C, I blew smoke rings and waved to the construction workers who would look up and wave back. My legs were thin and tan. I rubbed cocoa butter on them for hours. I painted my toenails light pink and stuck them out the window to dry. When Darren would get home I'd jump on him, wrap my legs around his waist, and kiss his neck. He'd give me some money and I'd make a few phone calls. That was my job, copping. I walked quickly to meet up with whoever called me back, always arriving early, and always having to wait. Sometimes I'd wait for ten minutes, and sometimes I'd wait for ten hours. It didn't matter if it was raining. It didn't matter that I hadn't eaten that day. It didn't even matter if I had enough money. After I copped I got a giddy feeling in my stomach, like the feeling before you get on a roller coaster. Sometimes I would get so excited I would throw up.

I'd run into the bathroom of any restaurant on Avenue A or 97th and Columbus or Mott and Prince or Orchard and Delancey. Then I'd do a few bumps in the bathroom stall and wait for the drip. I'd flush the toilet so no one would suspect anything, and then I'd bounce back onto the street. Light up a cigarette and go home to Darren where we would strip naked and stretch out on the bed, entangling our limbs like human pretzels while the dope rushed through our nervous system. For months we did that together, laboriously scratching our noses and cheeks. With our dopey eyes half-opened we made promises of love and children and a million other things that seemed just within our reach.

JULY 2000 · SUMMER-AGE 21

DEAR DIARY,
Tonight Darren and I got mugged. We were walking down Avenue B, one block away from his house on 7th street. This dude comes up behind me and grabs my bag and I just fucking chase after him and get all my shit back, I was so proud of myself. I got everything in my bag back except for $7, thank God because there was dope in there and my ID and all my phone numbers. Darren lost everything and I think he felt sort of stupid. I really need to stop doing

dope for a few weeks. My tolerance is just getting way too high. I gotta go cold turkey. I'm scared but I can get through it. I fucking love Darren so much.

UPDATE • This happened during summer break when Darren and I lived in Manhattan. All I cared about was dope. This is made especially clear in the above entry, where I risk my life by chasing down a bag. This is idiotic, especially in New York, but it didn't seem idiotic then; it seemed heroic and bad-ass. A few years after this a young woman named Nicole duFresne was coming home from Max Fish and got lippy with a mugger (not far from where Darren and I were mugged). He shot her in the chest and she died.

OCTOBER 2000 • 4TH YEAR OF COLLEGE-AGE 21

DEAR DIARY,

I am addicted to heroin. I don't know when it's going to stop. I miss Darren. We've always done dope together. When Darren and I stop, will the drugs stop too? Which will come first? If I quit, I know breaking up won't be far behind. I don't know what it feels like to love him 100% sober. I remember the first night we did dope. We were sitting out on the balcony right after I sniffed some and so did he. We left a bar early. It was something about him that triggered me and I kissed him on the cheek. He smiled. Before that, was I really interested? We went to the movies and he walked me halfway home. Gave me a crushed flower and kissed me on 14th and 2nd. We were sober. Just a summer before, on 14th and 1st, Brian broke my heart in 100 different pieces. Who knew?

NOVEMBER 2000 · 4TH YEAR-AGE 21

DEAR DIARY,

It's been 1 whole day without heroin. I feel like shit. It's only gonna get worse. It's good for me; I can be a normal person again. I can be myself. I can be happy. I miss Darren more than anything. It's a pain that never goes away. I think about him nonstop. I don't think I've ever loved anybody this much. This distance between us drives me crazy. I've done that drive so many times. 3 hours. Give or take a few minutes depending on traffic. What do I want to do with my life? I want to love him as a full-time job. I think this kind of yearning is worse than withdrawing from scag. I feel lost without Darren and dope. How can I find myself again? Without heroin everything is cold and everything hurts. It's boring. Depressing. You can't sit still. You can't sleep. You can't be happy. But what about before? Was the world like this before dope? I can't remember anything about myself before dope.

UPDATE · This is bullshit by the way. I hadn't quit at all. I kind of slowed down a bit but figured talking about it a lot would make it so. The only thing that really did make it so was going to rehab, and even then I tried to bail a few times.

Looking back, I only wish I hadn't put so much pressure on Darren. I wish I hadn't convinced myself that I needed him so much or even missed him or loved him. It was always about the drug. Always. And I was so fucking scared to admit that, so I made it seem like it was about Darren. I put him through a lot.

I managed to find Darren in Thailand of all places. He's working at some newspaper there so I contacted him on AIM. I hadn't spoken to him in 4 years.

Lesley: Hey Darren. What are you doing right now?
Darren: It's 10 AM here in Bangkok. I'm working.
Do you have time for a little chat?
Yes I got here early today. What did you want to ask me?
Have you stopped doing heroin?
Yes, completely.
When?
After you went to Betty Ford I had no more contacts and I dried out. I basically got pneumonia in the process of going cold turkey.
That's one cold turkey!
Ha ha! Yes. But yeah, I came out the other end a much stronger person. I think.
Do you think I made you do heroin?
Well . . . hmmm, that's hard. I mean, you didn't make me but it was kind of part of the package. It was like, I fell in love with you and at the same time, I fell in love with the experience of being with you on heroin. So you didn't make me but I was in love with the whole experience, you know what I mean? It was an implicit part of the whole experience.

Sometimes I wonder if we were ever really in love or if it was just the dope that made us think that.

I don't know. I never loved anyone since I loved you.

Wow.

Maybe it wasn't love, but I've never felt anything like that before.

I never really separated you and heroin.

Remember that time I was bawling my eyes out at that Irish restaurant?

No.

Hahaha. Oh man, I was a complete mess, like, "I can't live without you, blah blah blah . . . Don't leave me!" We were sitting outside at an Irish pub on Houston. You were like, "Oh really? It's OK . . ." but you were really detached.

I must have been high. Breakups are easy when you're high.
Ha.

I remember when I was in college; it was so hard for me to be without you. Sometimes I feel like I almost forced you to be with me. Like I dangled dope in front of you to get you to stay with me. And when we went cross-country I can barely remember what we did other than try to find drugs.

Really? I felt like . . . I felt like it was agony not being with you but dope was like an afterthought. That was a really weird trip.

I thought that after the trip you were like, "I'm over this." And after rehab it just faded. I don't even remember us breaking up.

Yeah, it was weird. I was doing dope, still sleeping at your house. I don't know. I mean, this is getting kind of personal but have you loved anyone since?

I always thought you were mad at me for making you do dope. And that your friends hated me . . . Yes I have loved since. I have been sober for years now. I have loved deeply and profoundly.

Is it really different?

What, being sober?

Loving. Being in love. Being in love sober, I guess.

Yes because it's not about our binge weekends when we wouldn't leave the bedroom for days. It's a lot harder and more complicated and just really different. It's not always about romance. But I have a much bigger capacity for love now. I am able to love my friends and family and have compassion for people I don't even know.

Hmmmm.

You just disappeared. I didn't know where you went. I assumed you thought I was just a huge waste of your time.

Isn't it strange the weird perceptions we get? I assumed you didn't want to be with me or talk to me afterward because I reminded you of your past and of drugs.

I guess I just didn't and still don't understand how someone who used so much heroin could just drop it and never go back. I thought you moved to Thailand to do dope!

Haha. You see, once you weren't on it, the attraction faded. I think more than half the fun of doing it was that I KNEW I would be with you on it! I don't know, I feel like . . . I feel like I don't know what love is. I mean, I love people but it's nowhere near the intensity I felt for you. I think the thing was I fell in love with you first, heroin second, and then things got confused.

I see. It's not like I really know what love is, though. I guess I know more about what love is not. For starters, it's not having to be on heroin together to have fun or be intimate . . .

Yeah that makes sense.

I think love is supposed to be awkward and hard and a process, I guess, not as immediate as it was for us. I can't just snap my fingers and be in love. On heroin it seems so intense but it's really just a great fucking high that gives you that facade. And I have loved deeply since, but that's not to say it worked; it didn't. We broke up. Love doesn't always "save the day" or whatever. But I do think it might make the world go 'round.

Wow. I guess I never thought of that—that love is supposed to be something difficult to handle.

Do you remember the last time you did dope?

The night before you left to go to California, I think. In your old apartment. I found some methadone you gave me once about a year later in an old backpack and did it. It was really strange, though.

What was it like?

My eyes were rolling into the back of my head and it sort of felt good but then I just felt weird. I felt dirty.

Did it feel like heroin?

Yeah, it did.

So the last night you did it we just sat in my apartment and got high, huh?

Yeah, you were like, "Stay over, let's do it one more time for old time's sake," or something like that. And I think we just sat in your apartment and did it. I think we might have had sex that night.

Did you think we would get back together after I got back from rehab? Did you want to?

No, honestly I didn't miss you because I finally got sober and realized that life was worth living again without heroin. Then I read that letter you sent to *Vice* and thought you resented me or thought I was a loser for being part of your life in some . . . lame role or something. That hurt. I felt stupid and I thought, "She doesn't want to talk to me anymore." So I figured I'd just move on.

Did I write something that specifically addressed you?

No, it was about rehab but you mentioned something about our last night together and I guess I interpreted it in a negative way.

I am so sorry if I made you feel bad. I just wasn't thinking about anyone other than myself.

Yes I know.

Do you drink or smoke weed these days?

Yes I do both but not in a crazy way.

And you NEVER come across dope? Come on, you're in Thailand!

I think there is dope here, but I'm not really tempted by it. And plus the drug rules here are WAY stricter. Like, a cop can come up to you on the street and strip-search you for no reason other than you are a foreigner. It's happened to me several times. Cops come into nightclubs, lock the doors, and piss-test the whole place!

It's serious, so there's the threat of jail to reinforce the antidrug thing.

Crazy! You know I have to say that even though my memory is clouded with heroin use, I know that I loved you. It was just so hard. Toward the end I was always doing it alone. It wasn't fun anymore. Kevin won't even talk to me. And he's sober now, like in NA and stuff. But you were and still are an awesome guy.

And you are still very sweet. I always think about Kevin when I put on my Saturday pants.

He got bad, started doing crack. He sold his car for like 4 bags of dope.

WHAT?

I wish he would talk to me, but what can you do?

You know I had a dream about you last night . . . I was trying to remember a song we always used to listen to . . . so strange . . . I can't remember what it was.

Oh! Try to remember! Was it Neutral Milk Hotel? "Game of Pricks"? "Trouble"?

That's the thing! I have this dream occasionally when we are hanging out and I say, "What was that song we always used to listen to?" and last night you handed me a John Cougar Mellencamp record, which I know is not it. Anyway, I gotta get back to work.

OK. Thanks for doing this.

Well, thanks for . . . I don't know. I feel really good to have said those things.

Me too! See you later sweet potater. Hit me up any old time.

I will.

NOVEMBER 2000 · 4TH YEAR-AGE 21

DEAR DIARY,
All I want to do is get fucked up fucked up fucked up
all I want to do is heroin. All I want is dope. I don't
want to write this dumb-ass assignment because all I
want is fucking heroin. Dope, heroin. Dope dope
dope dope dope dope. This assignment is not fun,
writing is not fun. I question if I still love it. I know
I used to love it. I was so passionate about it but now
what?!?! I can't stand this waiting waiting waiting I
need to get high right now Kevin where are you?!?!
Stop fucking around and get back here already.

UPDATE · Kevin and I used to play this game when either
one of us would go out to cop. Whenever we came back we'd
say something like, "I have bad news. Sasha didn't have any
left," or "I got mugged and lost everything," or "The cops
busted the place and I almost got arrested . . ." You get the
idea. Then we would say, "Surprise! JK!" and then we'd get
high. It was all really amusing and fun until the day came
around that one of us did get mugged, or the dude never
showed up, or the cops were there, etc. Then it became an
even bigger harsh bong hit. It's not a tactic I recommend for
drug users. It takes you about an hour to convince the guy
you actually really honestly don't have any dope this time.

DECEMBER 2000 · 4TH YEAR-AGE 21

DEAR DIARY,
While Darren and I drove to New Jersey tonight I

suddenly remembered how much ambition I used to have. Certain things were so important for me to see and do and now all those goals are gone. I used to want to see and do all kinds of crazy things. That used to be important to me. I wanted to take a train around the country and meet people and be a hippie. It's sad how sad I am. I liked it better in high school because in high school I was angry. More angry than sad and anger is such a strong, hard, passionate feeling. It is very alive whereas sadness is like floating. Being sad is like wanting to be nothing at all. I'm not afraid of growing up, I'm just afraid of getting older and growing down. I feel like there is more than one way of doing something and maybe this is just my path, the way I am supposed to do things. Maybe I'll just stop shooting up when it's time to get married and have kids. Why can't I think like I did when I was 17? It was all sex, love, punk rock, and sunsets.

UPDATE • When you're a junkie, you sometimes get to have moments of clarity like this. Unfortunately, the minute you start having these thoughts, getting high becomes a lot less fun. It became a battle I fought, in my head. The only thing that pushed aside my unhappiness was heroin. I even went to see a therapist during my last year of college, and her deal was that every time I did dope, I had to tell her. So every week, I told her I had done dope. It didn't change anything. I told her I needed it to relax, and she suggested that I replace

heroin with kava kava. Nice try. She was not the best therapist, but then again, I'm not sure she had much experience
with addiction. I don't blame her for not being able to "cure"
me; I blame myself for going to her in the first place. When
you have one foot in the heroin door and the other foot in
the regret-and-frustration door, you should just surrender to
the drug and wait to hit bottom. Try not to die in the process.

JANUARY 2001 · 4TH YEAR-AGE 21

DEAR DIARY,

Today on the plane I thought about the fact that I
didn't keep a record of my time in Austin but then I
turned into Jesse and thought: Travelogues are boring. I had a great time and I can remember. No need
to keep track of every restaurant I eat in, every boring detail about my life in a state other than New
York. I'm back home now and very high. It's not even
that great. I was sober for a week and I was fine. More
than fine, I had a great time. When I go back to
school I don't want to be fucked up every day. I want
to be a nice person again. I want to laugh with my
friends and write really good stories. I want to drink
coffee and get hyper. Drink tea. Smoke pot and watch
TV. I haven't spoken to Darlene in about a year, yet
she's invading my brain right now, teaching me to get
off on the world and stuff. I love the way a journal
looks. My own books filled up with the alphabet in
pretty black ink. It looks awesome. Words are so cool.
I love the physical act of writing. I like writing on

envelopes, other people's names in a nice way because it's so fun just to create a crazy style of lettering that totally reflects on the person you are. The way the letters hook on to each other. The T and the H and the E. There are so many pictures in my head that I want to somehow squeeze into these letters. So many things I feel that I want to throw across a page.

UPDATE · I was romanticizing the alphabet! That's the thing about junkies; they take the completely mundane and dream about it for hours. They fall in love with the cracks on the sidewalk, smile at the folds of a napkin, and wink back at the pile of shit that has a thousand eyes. In other words, they are mentally disabled. On acid you see your fair share of purple dinosaurs and pleated skies. On pot you get paranoid and hungry, and on coke you get addicted to more coke and talk about how much you love socks for 45 minutes straight. On heroin you are only one thing: boring. That's how you are to other people who are not on heroin. The only people who will tolerate you are the other junkies you are forcing yourself to hang out with. Eventually I get to the point where I just surrender to being a total fuckup, but there are a lot more boring entries on how I want to be a nice person and how great cardboard is.

MAY 2001 · 4TH YEAR-AGE 22

DEAR DIARY,
So I'm gonna be totally dope free this week. I flushed some down the toilet. I'll possibly feel shitty but I'll

deal with it. Valium and Tylenol PM, whiskey—fine. I already feel sick so hopefully I can just get everything out of me at once.

UPDATE · Trying to kick was sitting alone in the dark with a glass of straight whiskey gripped inside my white knuckles, and usually there were pills involved. It never lasted more than a few days.

Also this was during my college commencement, and I didn't even mention it. I knew I was going to move to New York, and I didn't think moving to New York after college was a big deal; I just assumed it was what everyone did. Same with graduating high school. I didn't think people had options. I didn't think that some people chose not to go to college, only that people either couldn't get in or couldn't afford it. I thought people who moved home after college were just losers. It never occurred to me that not everyone's parents helped support them.

I glossed over the milestones of graduating and moving to a new city. The truth is that I was numb to it all. I guess it felt good, but I know I was just told that it was supposed to feel good so that's how I said it felt at the time. "Good. Great. Awesome. I'm so glad we're done with school." Now that I'm older and not entirely mind-raped by the system, I think it all felt really sad. I had a delayed reaction, of course. I moved into an apartment on the Lower East Side of Manhattan, the first one I saw, and asked my mom for some rent and the broker's fee and money for cable and a phone and cell phone and "Don't worry, I'll get a job soon." But then I freaked out because suddenly I wasn't in Mod 100. This led to more heroin use and a credit card that I am still paying off today. Leaving college and that first year in New York were devastating. It was also really fun. It's the 22-year-old nervous breakdown that I hear is quite popular these days. The problem with going to a liberal-arts school and majoring in creative writing is that . . . you're fucked.

JULY 2001 · 4TH YEAR-AGE 22

DEAR DIARY,

I hate writing in my journal when I'm fucked up. It's so fake. I have this artificial yellow green glow all around me, inside me. I hate dope, I hate myself on dope. It's the same thing over and over. I'm a broken record. Things I like about me when fucked up:

- Really nice
- Find a boring conversation interesting
- Socially outgoing, less shy and insecure
- Affectionate more than usual
- Less inhibited to speak mind

UPDATE · In real life, when a conversation is boring, it means you shouldn't be having it. Unfortunately, the only thing I found boring back then was anything that didn't involve me. I mean, we're all selfish. We all enjoy it when people pay attention to us. Ever notice how amused people are when you point out one of their mannerisms or a funny quirk about them? They start laughing and getting happy because they're thinking, "People notice me! I'm relevant!"

It's OK to have these instincts, but you have to suppress them a bit. There are 6 billion people here, so it's not all about you. You need to let other people talk for a while and pay attention to their world for a sec. Heroin is all about the opposite. It's about saying, "Fuck the world this is about me," so you demand to be noticed. If people don't want to talk about you and your needs, they can go fuck themselves. Eventually, you have just one friend left: smack.

It's weird sometimes when I find myself in a conversation now and I'm actually interested in what the other person is saying. I'm actually listening to them, and I can feel the old junkie me saying, "Why do you give a shit about this bitch?" Junkie Me was a deadly combination of low self-esteem and a huge ego, which is also, guess what, boring.

THE DESCENT

SEPTEMBER 2001 · NEW YORK CITY-AGE 22

DEAR DIARY,

Today four Palestinians hijacked US airplanes. Two went straight into the Twin Towers. One went into the Pentagon and one got shot down or something. New York City is chaotic. Everything is shut down. World Trade Center is gone. I saw a million people walking over the Williamsburg Bridge. Subways are closed, Penn Station, etc. It's pretty fucking hectic. I can't find Darren and it's really starting to piss me off. He hasn't called since he went to 7th street and I don't know where he is. I can't get in touch with anyone, my phone is fucked up. I feel so tired, so sad, and so hungry. I have to call Freddy. Maybe I should just walk over there.

UPDATE · I woke up to see the first tower falling, and Darren and I went up on the roof to see the black smoke billowing up into the sky. People were scared and pissed. I didn't see a lot of fear around. Mostly rage.

Darren and I took to the streets to find something to eat

and a TV to watch the news. I saw two friends from college and sold them some shitty coke from the previous night. When Darren and I parted ways, the panic set in. Not panic about the fact that the East and West were now polarized. Not a panic about an imminent World War III. Who cares about that shit? I needed dope, and without cell phones working it was going to be really hard to hook up with Freddy, the dealer. I ran to the dealer's house and started pounding on his door. He was home. Thank god! After I got high I sauntered over to Max Fish, a bar on Ludlow, and calmly tried to figure out what the big deal was. Everyone was getting wasted. Some people were crying, but most of us were just glad to be there together. After that it was just booze and hugs.

I hope this doesn't reflect badly on New Yorkers. Mine was the junkie perspective, but most people were really cool to each other watching TV in bars and updating strangers on the latest info. I even saw a table of people at Doc Holliday's cheer when one of the guys found out his mother made it out alive. I was so out of touch with the human race that I felt embarrassed when they did that, or even when people cheered for the FDNY as they cruised down the streets. I felt like a little kid at a wedding, wondering why all the grown-ups were crying when the bride and groom kissed. I had no idea what I was feeling. I was scared to feel anything else but the numbness that was most familiar.

SEPTEMBER 2001 · NEW YORK CITY-AGE 22

DEAR DIARY,
Oh my God, what a fucking mess. Alvin meets us at

lunch—me and Michael and whoever—for his friend's B-day. Then later that night we meet at Max Fish. Take him home. Do dope with him and he's drunk. Darren "happens" to come by. FUCK. 7:30 AM Alvin starts dehydrating and his face turns blue and he starts vomiting after I make him drink water. 8:04 AM Alvin leaves, doesn't look very promising for our future together. I thought about Darren all night and how he probably hates me right now. It is not a time for me and boys. I give them dope. I am a disease. I feel like the sickest girl in the world. Someone should lock me up and put me away. I swear I thought this kid was gonna die here tonight. What would I have done? I don't even have salt or saline solution. I am so much better off alone it's scary. I know deep down I am OK but nothing ever counts deep down anyway, does it? I have to go now, go cut open my straw and scrape it. Luckily I have my silver straw around my neck. Surprised I haven't tried to cut that open. Surprised my nose is still attached to my face and that I haven't tried to cut that open and scrape it either.

UPDATE · Michael was one of my best buds for a while; he lived around the block from me, and we used to party together and hang out and sometimes do it. He was super-hot BTW. Eventually he moved to LA, but we still kept in touch. One night he was out with his friends doing coke and drinking, no big deal. Someone gave him an OxyContin and he took half. He may have had a seizure or something, but the next thing I know, I'm flying to LA to visit Michael in the hospital, he's been in a coma for a week. The doctors don't really know what happened, but something affected his brain in a really bad way. Michael had been interning at this hospital and studying for his MCATs. Now he lives with his parents and is relearning how to write. He just recently found out that he didn't have to wear his helmet anymore. I still talk to Michael sometimes, but he lives very far away and it's just . . . different.

Alvin is still my friend and recently got engaged. He is a photographer and lives and works in New York. I almost killed him. That's another thing about heroin. You end up introducing everyone you meet to it, and a lot of them end up dying. Alvin and Michael survived.

OCTOBER 2001 · NEW YORK CITY-AGE 22

DEAR DIARY,

I want to stop using but at this point I am afraid of getting sick. And because I have no job it's so easy to just go out and cop. NA seems like a really good thing. I think it could maybe help me one day. It's the kicking I'm afraid of, even with weed and Xanax. No boy prospects. Don't really care. Decided I want to hook up with an English guy but I don't know any. I wonder if Gavin can get me a job at *Vice*. Maybe I'll try to work at the library. When I finally get my shit together I'm gonna reward myself with a dog.

UPDATE · Darren and I broke up that fall. We drove around the country for about a month and half convincing ourselves that we would kick on the road. Turns out it was the dope that we were in love with, not each other, and we spent the entire trip just looking for drugs in other cities. We scored big in TJ and pretty much drove straight home after that. Our money was gone and we were all out of Aderall. If you ever want to break up with someone but you're not sure, go on a road trip together for at least 2 weeks. It's a good way to end a relationship because you won't feel sad, you'll feel relieved.

I couldn't find a job that allowed me to pursue drugs and being useless. Gavin hooked me up with an internship at *Vice*, which I fucked up and got fired from. Then they took me back as a freelance columnist, which is harder to get fired from because you only have to do one thing a month.

NOVEMBER 2001 · NEW YORK CITY-AGE 22

DEAR DIARY,
Mitch said he would pay me $900 a week if I kept their shit here and let him and Ross mix it here like one night a week. Seems like a good deal to me, because then I can intern and still be making money. Ross came over with this long-ass ecstasy belt—just like hundreds of pills to wear like a belt when you go to the airport or something. I'm sure he won't notice if a few are missing. This is crazy I know but whatever whatever whatever.

UPDATE · Ross and Mitch were two drug dealers I knew who came up with this idea to use my house as a base. They walked in one night with a few shoeboxes filled with cocaine and left it in the top of my closet. I promised myself I wouldn't dip into it. That promise lasted about a few hours. Before I knew it, my hands were covered in white powder, and because I had no scale I pretty much guessed how much a gram was. With coke all over my fingers and white dusty coke particles flying through the air, within a week I was hearing sirens. I heard sirens while I was in the shower, so I started showering with my sneakers and a set of clothes in the bathroom in case I needed to escape. I heard sirens in the back of the apartment, so I covered the walls with dark towels, sheets, and aluminum foil—I guess to block out the light and to pretend that whatever was out there waiting for me wouldn't be able to find me? I started hearing the cops knock on my door one terrifying day, so I pushed a big green chair in front of it. After a few hours I realized they weren't coming to get me and if they were they'd probably left. The paranoia wasn't the worst part, though. The worst part was that I actually started making a lot of money. At first it was great—I even bought a Chanel necklace and treated my friends to dinner and karaoke rooms. Eventually, though, my $10-a-day habit turned into a $50-a-day habit. I started to not dip into the coke and sell it but instead just trade it for the dope. The dream of making $900 a week did not exist in reality. Maybe Ross and Mitch knew I was stealing from them. One night as I was getting ready to go out, Mitch came in and told me he wanted to do some mixing (cutting the coke with laxative), but I was on my way out and told him to come back tomorrow. He got pissed and just took all the shoeboxes and went to a motel or something. The next day he was arrested. Turns out the cops or DEA or whatever had been watching him for months. Ross was taken in for questioning, but eventually the cops realized they had bigger fish to fry. They never even bothered with me. Or did they? Maybe all those sirens I had been hearing were real. Either way, Mitch is in jail today. I am not. Phew.

NOVEMBER 2001 · NEW YORK CITY-AGE 22

DEAR DIARY,

I am a smitten little kitten wearing mittens! Tonight I went to Lotus and saw Leo. I was all prepared to yell at him for "never saying hi to me" but then I remembered *The Girls' Guide to Hunting and Fishing* and thought, "I'm gonna do the opposite tonight and just be fucking humble." And then Leo came over to me and we talked and talked and then he got up but he came back! And we talked some more. And I was the one to leave first. Michael said it was a really good sign that he came back because he had friends all over the bar and he could've gone over and talked to them but he decided to talk to me (although he did leave his jacket on the chair . . .). Anyway he's really awesome and down to earth, not at all like an actor. He doesn't seem like the kind of guy who really kicks it to girls. I hope I don't blow it by being so forward, too eager and too obvious. I hope I see him tomorrow night at Spa.

UPDATE · I had a huge crush on Leo Fitzpatrick, the funny-toothed actor you may remember from *Kids*. We hooked up once and realized we were not soul mates. Maybe I should have given him heroin. Today we are buds.

JANUARY 2002 · NEW YORK CITY-AGE 22

DEAR DIARY,

It's not even like they try to make recovery look fun. A million pamphlets that say the same things in different words fanned out on my bed. Mustard, bone, pea—the colors of recovery. Basic blue, dirt brown. No outstanding kind of gold. You would think that because of the importance of these words they would plate them in gold or something, but no. It says, "Talk to God, ask God, submit yourself and kneel to God . . ." How? What's God? If my lack of excellent prose is not enough to keep me sober, then nothing is. Not even God. I'm afraid.

UPDATE · I started going to NA meetings during this time, always high, if not before the meeting, then immediately after. The books I read talked about having to get a higher power in order to stay clean, so I went around asking all the people at the meeting what their higher power was. Didn't get too many straight answers. Unless I just don't remember because I was so fucked up. But going up to people and saying, "Hi. What's your higher power?" is weird. Even at NA.

JANUARY 2002 · NEW YORK CITY-AGE 22

DEAR DIARY,

All my jeans are too fucking big which is ridiculous because they are either a size 2 or a waist of 26. Today I ate a croissant with ham and cheese, Twizzlers, and a hot dog. I'm dehydrated and underweight and it's noticeable. Tony's count just seems to keep getting lower and lower and his shit shittier. Or is it me? Either way, it's ridiculous and it's MY fault! My decision to keep using. Broke again and in debt, my mom keeps asking why I'm spending so much money. My sister looks at me funny. Don't they know? Can't they fucking tell? At this point if they asked, maybe I would just tell them. I know I would. Do they know but don't want to believe it? I need pills to kick but I need the will to want the pills. It's a fucking circle. I want to stop. I'm sick of this shit, the money, the copping, the everyday drag of maintaining, the sickness. It's annoying yet the first thing I think of in the morning is the shot I have to prepare myself for. Sometimes it takes too long to get it ready and I just need a line to get into the bathroom. There is so much bullshit I need to take care of: getting the cat spayed, getting my guitar back (Austin probably sold it by now), writing a piece for Steve Lafreniere (that shouldn't even be a stress-related thing). Kevin is coming on Friday and it's just another excuse for me not to kick. The thing is, I don't even like getting high with other people anymore. I like being alone and doing it alone. I wish Champ would just crawl into my arms right now but Dr. Diaz said I have to let her come to me.

UPDATE • I used to make deals with myself. Like, "If I get my apartment really clean, it will help me want to quit dope," or "If I get a cat, I will have to quit doing dope because I want to be a good parent." Champ was the first pet I had ever owned. Not only did I not get clean, but realizing the responsibility of taking care of an animal made me want to get even more fucked up because I didn't really know what I was doing. Today Champ is alive and well, purring like a lil' angel. At least she's not watching me shoot up anymore.

FEBRUARY 2002 • NEW YORK CITY-AGE 22

DEAR DIARY,

I am so fucking depressed. I don't even know how to write anymore. I haven't written anything in so long. I hate going out. All I do is stay home, do dope. I stopped answering my phone because I can't stand the sound of my own voice lying. I feel like I have a black cloud over my head, always. I am afraid of my own words and am living in my own hell. I want to be myself again. To write again. To be clean and OK but every time I try I fail. I want to die. I feel entirely empty and scared and gutless. I am killing myself. I understand why I have no friends; I'm not even me anymore. I want to tell my mom but I am so fucking scared she will help me. Why am I so afraid to get help? There's a void in my heart. I feel no soul, no emotion, nothing. I don't even hate myself because I don't even feel angry enough to hate anything. I wish it was hate. I just want to be someone else, somewhere else; I can't remember a time in my life when I didn't want that. I want to get better but don't have enough strength to do it on my own. I want to crawl inside my mom and stay there for 9 more months. I have no love to give anyone, no love inside me, all I feel is the constant drip in the back of my throat or the dull throbbing pain in my vein.

UPDATE · Darlene had called my mom and told her I was a junkie, but my mom didn't believe her because Darlene was a Jehovah's Witness and therefore not a reliable-enough source. Looks like she could have used Jesus on her side, because I was practically begging to be found out. I called my mom a few days later and told her everything. I wanted to go home and take Valium and have her tickle my arm for a few days while I kicked, then go back to my apartment and be all better. My mom had other plans.

FEBRUARY 2002 · REHAB #1-AGE 22

DEAR DIARY,
Well, here I am in detox at South Oaks. I don't even know how to comprehend the past 48 hours. I called the *Vice* dudes and left a message and I know I should call my mom but I am kind of pissed at her. And I am afraid to call Leigh and Kevin and Darren.

It is so fucking strange here. I don't really know what to do with myself. But here I am. It makes me think of that one chick from the hardcore scene that went crazy one year and stayed here. It makes me think of bulimic girls from high school and kids who started doing heroin when they were, like, 10. It reminds me of Sam too. Kids with social problems. I think I only want to be here for 3 days. Is 3 days enough? I still feel like if I could do dope right now, I would. I don't want to of course but I still don't understand how all of this figures out and fits together. The people here are all older and scary. There is this woman who is like 300 pounds and she's a crackhead and in a wheelchair and I think she shits her pants!!! Some people are nice but they are such Long Island trash. But I guess that's what I am too. I guess I'm proud of myself for not crying. I think if I'm here and I see this kind of stuff I will NEVER want to come back here again. I still feel like I'm on dope, in a haze. Like all this stuff is going on and it hasn't hit me yet. Thank God for methadone. The group meeting was so funny. These 2 women started fighting, they're roommates. The one girl was like, "She keeps chicken in her room!" And the other one was like, "So? You smoke in the room!" And then they were voting for President, V. Pres, secretary and it was so fucking funny because no one could figure out how to vote. I had to cover my mouth to keep from laughing out loud. I keep

thinking about Jesse and how he said, "Don't worry,
this will all make a good story one day."

UPDATE · The 300-pound woman was Jerri, a crackhead
who had fully given up on life. When she entered rehab she
was wheezing, smoking, sitting in a wheelchair, and eating a
meatball sub. She was incapable of wiping her own ass, literally. I thanked God I was not a nurse and prayed to sweet
Jesus that she would NOT be my roommate. Her skin was
gray. She beefed like a trumpet teacher, and you could hear
her wheezing through the dormitory walls.

Once, during my methadone stint, I offered to wheel her
around. I wasn't strong enough to move her one fucking
inch. She was total dead weight. Then one day, after a meal, a
nurse told Jerri she could not smoke indoors. She got right
up out of her wheelchair, walked outside, and lit up a Kool.
The nurses were furious. Jerri could walk. She was fully capa-
ble of getting around on her own but chose to wheelchair it
because she "didn't feel like walking." The bitch was that lazy!
Seeing her waddle outside to smoke that cigarette was the
first time I'd felt an emotion in almost a decade (it was a little thing called anger).

During family week Jerri's son came. He was my age and
kind of thugged out, but when he started crying I knew I
was in for more than I could handle. He really wanted her
to get help. He was ashamed of his mother. Meanwhile, all
105 pounds of me was bopping around on methadone
wearing Marc by Marc Jacobs jeans, counting down the
minutes to when I could stop yessing everyone and just get

the hell home. I was done withdrawing now. After six days I was better.

DEAR DIARY,

My heart is beating fast and I feel like I can't catch my breath. I don't know what's wrong with me. It's hard getting used to this new life. I really don't know why I can't breathe or eat or do anything. I don't know what to do. Shower? Try to eat? Watch TV and try not to think about it? I feel restless but exhausted. This apartment is cold and messy. My stomach is so tight and I wish it would go away. Is it the obsession? I want it to be lifted. I DO NOT want to call Tony and use. By the grace of God please watch over me today and help me stay clean.

DEAR DIARY,

Good news! I remember Suroosh mentioning something about bringing back all the old columns *Vice* used to do like "DEAR DIARY," and "Ask the Farm." It dawned on me that I have all my old diaries and that I could possibly do the column. So I mentioned it to Gavin and he thought it was a good idea. He told to write one and if it was good they'd put it in. It's so fucking perfect I can't even deal. I'm almost not even that surprised because it just seems so right, like it was just meant to be and that's that.

UPDATE • Suroosh is another guy who started *Vice*. I knew him for a long time before finding out he used to be a junkie, a bad one, for five years. After months of sneaking off to the bathroom to get high every hour, I approached Suroosh and asked him what I should do. It was awesome to hear that someone who used to steal cars and basically killed his best friend was now in charge of a company. Suroosh took me out for pizza, and we traded war stories. I told him I didn't know how to get clean and that I couldn't go back to rehab because "I had to show up for my internship at *Vice*." Suroosh kindly let me know that the office would survive without me. My dad later thanked him in an e-mail for introducing me to the concept of rehab, a concept that, eventually, saved my life.

APRIL 2002 • NEW YORK CITY-AGE 23

DEAR DIARY,

I just totally remembered my MO for going to detox. I remember thinking that I wanted to get my tolerance back so that I wouldn't have to spend so much money. Wow, right? I actually remember thinking that "no, I don't need help staying clean, I only need help kicking." Interesting turn of events some might say. Someone else might not say that at all, however. If I were to get high right now, I would vomit. But then what? Nothing. A great feeling of immense nothingness followed by a series of nothings. Really. It would feel good, I guess but my idea of "good" is not the same anymore. I do not equate numbness with "good" right now. Later, maybe, but right now I really don't. Been thinking more about other vices lately. Jack and coke, Johnny Walker Black Label on ice, white Russian. Basically all Irish whiskey, all creamy and soft and white, like my belly. I don't want to be an alcoholic! I'm already an addict, so isn't that enough? I don't even know how to spell it: alcoholic . . . is that right? I think about summer and 40s and blunts. It would be cool to go on a cross-country tour of meetings. Darren and I did a cross-country tour of bars and cop spots and it was hard and frustrating. I want to do it again and I want to do it different. I want to do it right this time.

APRIL 2002 · NEW YORK CITY-AGE 23

DEAR DIARY,

I spent all day at Terry's. His life is exciting and he was married to a model and he is friends with all sorts of celebrities and is sort of a celeb himself, yet he tells me that I'm his favorite person and he calls me on my cell after chilling with me all day and tells me that I'm awesome. "Stay clean," he says. I don't know what to do with these things because I can so easily let them get to my head. For me, boys come right after drugs, my second-favorite vice. And boys won't kill me like drugs will.

UPDATE · I hung out with photographer Terry Richardson during my first days of sobriety. We had a lot of fun eating sandwiches and chain-smoking. Most of the time I was just there, sitting around while models got naked and did splits for him, or maybe Vincent Gallo was doing something "wacky" for the camera. My mind was totally blown. But the mask of glamour only lasted so long before I started to get jealous. Terry was rich and successful. I was not. The models were skinny and beautiful and got paid for it. I was different. I started to compare our lives, which is ridiculous considering the life he's led.

I started to feel like the token ugly girl, sitting around, picking the cheese off my pizza, pretending to watch *The Sopranos* while some string bean of a girl was sitting on Terry's lap feeding him grapes. It was too much for me. It wasn't Terry's fault; it was mine. I couldn't handle it. Today Terry and I are friends; but it's different. When I relapsed I called him and freaked out on him. Considering he's the most unconfrontational dude, it was a bad move.

MAY 2002 · NEW YORK CITY-AGE 23

DEAR DIARY,

Tonight the meeting I went to was held outside. There were no slogans posted up. I miss Darren sometimes. I miss doing heroin with him and staying up all night talking. We talked and cried and died and prayed and promised and fucked and smoked and held each other tight until the sun came up. I miss that. I miss the way he always woke up smiling. I miss the way we would fuck, sometimes while we were still asleep even. There was never any sleeping.

Just that weird heroin state of in-between. Those lucid nightmares. I miss the way he used to talk in his sleep. I dreamt that someone had broken into his apartment while we were watching TV in his room. I miss that room. In that room, Darren was still in love with me. I think we both knew it would end after our road trip. I remember that night we were high, in my bed, deciding to break up and then the plastic jelly bracelet that said "Wear this for as long as I love you" broke. I wanted to cry but I was too fucked up. I just did another line. Once he described heroin as an artificial glow and sometimes that description was almost too perfect. But other times that glow seemed as natural as the blood running through me. As natural as every cell in my brain, or every dream I've ever had. I miss heroin and I miss Darren and I miss them both together. In the end, he only loved dope. He only came around for the heroin. He even stole my heroin! I was just the middleman. I wonder where he is? Sometimes I just can't believe this life I'm in right now. Where am I and who is this person lying in my bed? Why can't I sleep at night and who ate all my drugs? Where is my dope and where is my boyfriend and where did all of that time go? All of a sudden my heart feels broken. A dull pain, sort of like a sunburn all over my body. Things still hurt.

ROCK BOTTOM

JUNE 2002 • NEW YORK CITY-AGE 23

DEAR DIARY,
What happens when you fuck up? When you fall off your bike or the record skips when you DJ? What happens when you make a mistake?
Nothing.

I've been thinking about relapsing lately. Thinking a lot about relapse more and more. For the most part I am just craving a drink but then sometimes it's coke and tonight—tonight its dope. Fuck. The thing is, I'm not doing anything to change it. I'm not calling my sponsor, not doing step work, I don't even make meetings like I used to. It's like I've already relapsed in a sense and now I'm just waiting for the perfect time. There is no perfect time. Nobody really cares what I do anyway and if they do, it's none of their business. I feel so fat. I hate going to the gym. My parents are fucking getting a divorce and it fucking hurts. I used to really believe that love could last forever because they really seemed to make it work. It didn't work. I have little inspiration for anything these days. I don't want to go back to where I was with dope, I really fucking don't. But I want to not care about anything again like I used to. I want to be thin again. I felt so beautiful on dope. Right now I feel nothing for no one and I don't want to exist. I hated being dope sick. It was the worst thing ever. But today I fucking hate NA. I hate everything. I don't know why. I just do. I feel so huge and all I want to do is disappear.

My heart; I want it gone. I want to break things but I can't break things anymore. I hate myself still. I hate myself for not being the person that people want me to be. I want to be perfect to everyone but I also just want to go back to the bar.

UPDATE • I associated being sober with being "good." I thought that if I stopped doing drugs and stopped drinking, I would have to surrender to being a loser. Sitting home on Friday nights and doing needlepoint (though I have done that once or twice). I thought being clean would turn me into a nerd, always nice to everyone, fake happy. If anything it's the opposite, but I didn't know that then. When sober people told me, I didn't want to believe them. I thought everyone was full of shit, including me, so fuck it? Why not get loaded?

JUNE 2002 · NEW YORK CITY-AGE 23

DEAR DIARY,

I relapsed at Darlene's wedding; wine and a beer. The next night at John Street I did coke. I don't feel guilty but I have to tell people I guess. I don't want to start my day count over or go to meetings. I don't want to work the program. I don't want to do heroin but I never wanted to stop EVERYTHING, even from the beginning. I think I can not be a heroin addict and still drink and do drugs and be OK. I'm not sure I'm an addict. No more than anyone else in this world. I don't want to be programmed. I never wanted to be an addict and I never wanted to surrender. Sorry!

UPDATE · Darlene had a Jehovah's Witness wedding where they made an announcement not to tap glasses with your fork because that invites the evil spirits in. They did encourage drinking, however. My reasoning at the time was, "If the JW's can drink, then so can I!" That was all it took. My parents had recently split up and had the gall to say, "Since you were so honest with your life, we decided to be honest with ours." Nice one. It's my fault. I was looking for an excuse, and that one was almost too perfect. The coke the next night? Well, John Street was a really fun party downtown, and I went every weekend sipping my Diet Coke. That Friday I had a real drink in my hand. Then I saw Vincent give a little nod and go into the bathroom, and I realized that that's where I wanted to be. I was never good at just sitting at the bar sipping a cocktail. I wanted to be in that bathroom.

My whole world existed in that tiny bathroom stall. It's the ultimate VIP lounge, and that was where I wanted to be seen going into, and it was where I wanted to be seen coming out of. I needed to get back in there. That was home.

JUNE 2002 · NEW YORK CITY-AGE 23

DEAR DIARY,
I ate 2 Percocet last night and puked twice. I was at Leigh's. She gave them to me. I did not enjoy vomiting at all. I was high but I didn't want to be. It didn't feel that good. The thought of doing dope scares me and excites me simultaneously. I went to a meeting today but left early.

UPDATE · It seems pretty obvious that one would not enjoy vomiting, but up until that point I actually did enjoy it. When I puked on dope or even pills, coke, or mushrooms it felt good because it meant that it was working, and I liked it when it worked. It was when I didn't puke from dope that I knew there was a problem. That meant it had been cut or that my tolerance was getting higher. Puking was good because it made me feel like I was still new and naive and couldn't handle the high. It made me feel like I wasn't addicted.

JUNE 2002 (6:01 AM) · NEW YORK CITY-AGE 23

DEAR DIARY,
So fucking high on coke and booze. Stacey and Meghan, all night with them, fun, fun. Chance wants nothing to do with me. Fine. I know I don't really

care anyway. I can't believe how fucked up I get and I think dope is my only problem. It's so not. I get drunk and I must do coke. The next thing I know I'm puking because I can't swallow a Tylenol 3. Gag reflex. Coke does not make me wanna fuck. Sleeping all day, missing the sun. I know I don't want that. But I party and when I party I do it hard. Too hard! I didn't think it would be like this. I thought it would just be margaritas but I haven't had one margarita, just bourbon and coke. Cocaine. It's getting out of hand

already. Aron, Kid America, Eric—they say they care but they don't. Ryan and Amy—I believe them. But it's about me. It's about going out and being a part of everything. I'm an addict but I really, really don't want to be. This is insanity. I can hardly breathe without a cigarette. It's not like it was before with Darren, in bed all day and night. It's different. It's like high school. Right now I'm alone and I wanna be.

SEPTEMBER 2002 · NEW YORK CITY-AGE 23

DEAR DIARY,
I don't understand why I feel the need to destroy:
My face
My body
My head
My heart
I'm going backwards in time. It's not fun anymore. Was it ever fun, or was I faking that? Confusing experience with self-destruction. Selling myself out for a few stories that I'll never tell because they're too boring. I'm just replaying someone else's story and not in a good way. I feel like I've been going in circles my whole life. Spending so much time looking for the party but never actually being there. Once, I found the party, it sucked. Went looking for another one. They're all the same. I keep hurting myself and that ain't no party. I've gotta get over Chance and that whole crew. It has to happen. I don't want my whole life to be NA/AA it doesn't have to be. I don't have to

live black and white, all or nothing. Emily assumed I'd flake on helping her and I did. Why? Because I didn't want to miss out, just in case something extraordinary happened. Like what? Chance sleeping over? He doesn't want to anymore. Fucking accept it. What did I give up $125 for? Some blow and Max Fish, dope. It's driving me deeper and deeper away from everything. I was once OK without dope and it came back. They were right. Drinking opened up the gate. I fucked myself. I need to go away, maybe upstate somewhere to kick and once I kick it's straight to NA because I cannot do this again! It was too hard the first time and I never wanted to do it again. How did I forget so easily? It's easy to kick. Staying clean is the hardest thing in the world. But I want to try again, I really do. I need to stop this bull-shit, this phase has to end. Everyone is worried. They should be. I'm a mess and I can't show up for any-thing. I want to be responsible again. This shit isn't even that good. I'm alone with it. There's no Darren, it's just me. Thank God for that. I want to know why I hate myself. I want to know why I love to destroy myself, my face. My skin is so bad I'm embarrassed and I keep doing it. I can't stop picking when I'm fucked up. It almost feels good to hurt myself more. And that is why Chance doesn't want to sleep over. He doesn't want to wake up next to the girl who has the chicken pox. I don't blame him. I don't want to be this girl anymore. This girl sucks. We hate each other.

OCTOBER 2002 (8:50 AM) · NEW YORK CITY-AGE 23

DEAR DIARY,

I can't believe I'm still awake and that I keep doing this when I have shit to do. The best part of last night was talking and dancing with Kathleen Hanna at the Hole. She was always my ultimate girl hero and she told me that I was awesome and she didn't want me to die because I have to write one day and that I might write something that changes her life and she needs me to stay alive for that reason. I want to believe her, even if she never remembers me. I feel like she was telling me things I already knew but never wanted to believe. We are really similar, all the things she was saying, it sounded like shit that would come outta my mouth although I'm sure every girl that likes her thinks that. She made me want to write again. I want to get off this shit that makes the pen stop working and my hands stop moving. It's time.

UPDATE · Bikini Kill was my favorite band because a) they fucking killed, doye, and b) Kathleen Hanna had the kind of energy that I was always attracted to. She was a bad ass, and her lyrics were smart and funny, and in interviews she would talk about feminism and punk and all these really smart things, but she talked just like me. She talked about politics and sex and music in a way that was really unpretentious and approachable, and I absorbed everything she said. I went to see Bikini Kill play when I turned 18 or 19, and Kathleen handed out her fanzine, *April Fool's Day*, about her journey to get sober. She explained that she had been abusing her body for years and was ready to start taking care of herself and that treating your body well and doing things without getting fucked up was punk too. This was the first time I really took notice of someone who was able to not get wasted and stay cool. Before that, I had only known militant straightedgers who were unhappy and mean and basically just needed a drink. They got high off of thinking they were better, and I wasn't interested in that vibe at all. Kathleen wrote fun top-ten lists of things that are better when you're sober, like listening to Elvis Costello and the moon in Texas. I always remembered that, and even though I continued to get fucked up for a few more years, I will always remember that weird little nod of approval I needed from my role model. Today Kathleen isn't really my hero anymore, only because I'm older and don't have many heroes besides myself, but the ghost of what she and her music meant to me still shows up from time to time when I get really fucking angry. As a woman, I felt as though she had given me permission to feel that way.

REHAB
FOR REAL

✷

OCTOBER 2002 • REHAB #2-AGE 23

DEAR DIARY,

Haven't really felt much like writing. Yesterday was hell. Starting to feel a little bit better physically. I guess this is the best place for me to stay although I really wish I was back at South Oaks. The people were just too funny there. The women here are all lame. Like proper and prim and dorky and don't seem like drug addicts at all. The guy thing bothers me but it's probably for the best. Ultimately I am here for myself and I know that but homework and working out—ugh. I feel unmotivated and still kind of depressed. I want to feel good and be happy. I guess I wonder what's going on in New York but not really. Same old shit, I know. I wish there was just 1 person that I truly loved here. Ramie is so young and very annoying but she means well.

UPDATE · I consider this my real bottom. This wasn't a financial bottom because I had been working at a vintage clothing store and making money. It wasn't a social bottom because I knew I had friends who loved me. It was a spiritual bottom. It dawned on me one day that my heart just wasn't in it anymore. It seems funny, but I remember watching Mary J. Blige sing during an awards show or something, and she kept thanking God for her life and for her success. For a moment I considered this: What if God really had helped her? What if God was responsible for her success? I heard all these hip-hop people constantly thanking God and they were all really rich and seemed happy. For a second I was like, "Dang son. Maybe God is a real G." The moment passed and I didn't remember that again until years later, but now I wonder if thinking that for a split second actually meant something truly monumental. My heart was breaking, and heroin was the culprit. I knew I wanted things in my life, like marriage and babies and careers. I knew that planning my entire day around when I needed to get high just wasn't going to get me any of those things. My tolerance had also gotten pretty high at that point, and it wasn't working like it used to. It stopped being fun. I was over it.

When I wanted to go to rehab I called my mom and told her I was ready and would she help me get back into South Oaks? A friend of a friend of hers had gone to the Betty Ford Center, so when she mentioned that place and asked if I would go there, visions of palm trees and Robert Downey Jr. danced in my head. I was still high when I made the decision, but I made it anyway. I think that's called Grace. I decided to totally indulge myself and do as much heroin as I could before. I had already committed to a date, so why not live a little before I go? That's what people do before they go to jail, right? On the plane I sniffed a bundle and barely got high. I knew it was just over. I gave up. It wasn't about being broke or not having any friends; it was that my soul was dying.

OCTOBER 2002 · REHAB #2-AGE 23

DEAR DIARY,

The thing about BFC is that they get really good speakers. This woman spoke tonight and her basic message was about selflessness, doing things for other people. She said when she did things for others; her obsession to use/drink went away. She talked a lot about God's will and how he wanted her to live because she believes that even when she was trying to die, she didn't—which is a lot harder. Trying to die is a lot harder than trying to live; it's a lot more painful. For the first time in my life I'm imagining having kids, having a life. A future. New York takes on a whole new personality for me each day. I loved partying there but I know what comes after the party. Lots of bullshit. Fashion, art, looking cool. Everyone there thinks they're part of this huge happening that's being documented and it's starring them. It seems so empty to me. I've always just wanted to: write, get published, fall in love, laugh a lot. That's pretty much it. Seems harder than it sounds.

UPDATE • This was written after I kicked, which sucked. They don't call it "cold turkey" for nothing. I'm serious. The phrase comes from heroin withdrawal symptoms. You get goose bumps like turkey skin, even if it's 90 degrees out. "Kicking" isn't just a cute way of saying it either, because your legs really do this involuntary kick from muscle spasms. It gets so hurty that you turn into a child having a temper tantrum. Counselors in rehab describe it as "musical chairs" because after you sit in one place and feel like you finally might be able to chill the fuck out, the kick starts creeping up, and you move to another chair. After you've covered every chair in the room, you surrender to the toilet, the only chair that will open its jaws for the massive amounts of diarrhea you're gonna get. Be sure to shit with a bucket in your lap, because all those years of dopamine reactors blocking the pain that you're supposed to feel when, let's say, you get a paper cut, are now coming out ten times stronger. It's like there's a barf-filled firehose in your mouth, pointing out. This is your body reacting to you being a total asshole to it.

When group therapy starts, things get a lot worse. That's when the real pain kicks in. Barfing and shitting are nothing compared to taking a "personal inventory" (a written list of all the ways you're a totally worthless turd). Physical opiate withdrawal only lasts five days.

OCTOBER 2002 • REHAB #2-AGE 23

DEAR DIARY,
It felt really good to share at the meeting tonight

because the speaker asked me to close the meeting and it made me feel really good.

I just pray and hope that I never forget this detox. It was worse this time. I begged nursing every day for methadone. I went early to meds every night, not because it was one of my only chances to see the boys but because I couldn't sit still. Kicking is like moving from one chair to the next to the next. This last run, I knew I'd be back in rehab, so I just figured I'd up the ante and do as much dope as I could before I was ready. My habit progressed so quickly because I just assumed that BFC would hook me up with the best meds.

I was sadly mistaken.

I remember Stacey, the counselor, coming into my room. I was in my bed and she came to talk to me. I couldn't stop moving my feet, my legs hurt so much that I couldn't stop kicking them, pounding them on the bed. It was the only time I ever considered cutting myself because I needed to release something so badly—something other than diarrhea every ten minutes. The only thing I could do was wait 4–7 days. 4–7 days! I refused to unpack my bags. I needed to leave. Coming here was my decision but it wasn't a sober one. When I finally landed I felt like I was in a really bad dream. I wanted a shotgun. I wanted to die.

Now I've been here. I don't want to die. Today there is no turning back.

UPDATE · Going to Betty Ford was the best, the worst, the strangest month of my entire life. The first thing I did was write a letter to my pals at *Vice*, which they ended up printing without my permission. It went like this . . .

Dear VICE,

Yo douche bags, what's the haps? I am literally writing from the infamous Betty Ford Clinic. You would not believe this place. You just would not fucking believe it. It's been four days for me, seeming more like four months. People come, people go, some people run away, and some don't ever want to leave. Two days ago my bags were pretty much packed and I was ready to bolt to LA and fly home, but I'm actually considering doing the 28 days now. I feel so far away from home. I get so sad when I think about New York and you guys and my mom. I realize my decision to come here was not a sober one, and the repercussions were a lot more intense than I had ever imagined. One thing that really bothers me is that the boys and girls aren't 'sposed to "fraternize," which is so different from the last place I was in.

The last place, South Oaks, was fucking awesome. Everyone there was mandated and had missing teeth and were hiding chicken in their bedrooms. Everyone there was a junkie.

Everyone here however was into booze + pills mostly, the occasional meth-head, a handful of coke heads. I think me, this dude Kevin, and this chick Lisa are maybe the only junkies. Can you imagine? You guys would hate it here. Everyone is normal. I'm still here. Haven't left yet. Wouldn't be opposed to getting kicked out but there is no dude who is worth it. My mom's heart is breaking and I really want to get better so I guess I'm staying. Yes. I'm staying.

I guess I just want to learn how to be happy + stop hating myself so much. Gavin, you are a hypocrite for doing dope with me at Christmas, but you're also an alcoholic so fuck you (JK—sort of). I want to write books. I wanna do stuff. I fucked Mark the night before I came. We got high 2gether. It was nice but I know when I'm not fucked up I think he's boring. I'm so bored right now. Withdrawing from dope w/out methadone SUCKS!

I know I'm doing the right thing though. It's beautiful here. I'm in the desert, there are mountains all around. The weather is in the 80s but it's dry and comfortable. I'm going to be starting a whole new life when I get back; a real one. That's going to be rad.

Peace + what not,
Lesley
Betty Ford, CA

Rehab is basically boredom, farting, and terrible roommates. There is nothing to do in rehab. That's the way it goes, and it goes that way for a reason. Boredom will drive you to participation, and the more you engage, the more you learn about sobriety. Most addicts are socially fucked to the extreme and can barely have a conversation, much less a friendship or a relationship. Boredom helps you get out of your room and make some buds. It's either that or trying to stare a hole through your bedroom wall.

A typical rehab day consists of eating, AA/NA meetings,

eating more, group therapy, smoking, more eating, more AA/NA, smoking and eating, and sleep. Getting crushes on ugly people is another activity.

Farts are huge there. Everyone farts all the time. Maybe it's all the coffee or maybe it's part of your body getting back on track. I've noticed hangovers include a lot of farting. People fart so much that the farts actually have their own conversations with each other. They have their own underground society and their own rules. Some farts even hate each other's guts.

Once you get over the farts and boredom you're stuck with roommates. I had this one lady everyone called "Tomato on a Toothpick" because she was really skinny but had a huge red face (broken capillaries from drinking). She also talked like a robot and asked every day if she could wear my clothes (just inappropriate—she was 55). Then I had this other lady who would never fucking shut the fuck up and, when anyone else spoke, did that annoying thing that people who don't listen do—nodding her head real fast with her eyes closed, like "Yup, yup, I know what you mean." She farted constantly in her sleep, and showered and shat with the door open. I even walked in on her masturbating! Ew!

OCTOBER 2002 · REHAB #2-AGE 23

DEAR DIARY,
I can do this. I can do this. I can do this. I can do this. I know I can do this.

UPDATE · By the end of rehab I still couldn't really eat anything except fruit because it was cold, wet, and sweet. I don't know why this happens when you kick dope, but you crave sweets and can barely eat solid food. So I was sitting in the cafeteria with Ramie but also just being antisocial and scared and silent. I looked down at my bowl and picked up a perfect strawberry. It was like a cartoon drawing of a strawberry. Red, seeds all symmetrical, a perfect triangular shape. Pretty little green leaves on the top like a fancy hat. I looked at that strawberry for a good five minutes and wondered how it could be so perfect. Who made it? It came from the dirt? How can anything taste this fucking good? Suddenly this fruit I had known my entire life became alien.

I looked at the berry. The berry looked at me. Boom, just like that, but quiet and obvious. I was different. Like most things I would look at after that moment, I saw something beyond what it actually was. It was still a strawberry but it wasn't *just* a strawberry. It was God. When I realized that, my heart stopped a little. Maybe it was something I had always known, because it didn't hit me like a realization, but more like a reminder. I have to admit that everything became a little bit easier after that. Things were going to be different now.

When I was done with Betty Ford I went back to New York and slowly got my life back together. I stopped talking to the people I did drugs with and got a job.

NOVEMBER 2002 · NEW YORK CITY-AGE 23

DEAR DIARY,
Today I left BFC. I saw three rainbows on the way to the airport. Three! Apparently not only am I sober, I'm also a leprechaun. All the girls came outside to

give me hugs and say good-bye. I dropped my luggage and ran over. I'm sad. I'm going to miss this place. Truly. Last time I was on this plane I used heroin in the bathroom. I felt antsy and uncomfortable the whole time. I am a bit nervous/scared to go back to New York only because I don't know what's in store but that's life. I'm not used to it. I think I would like to work with teenagers one day. Teenage boys, an all-boys private school. Ha ha. Now that I'm off drugs I guess you can say I'm pretty horny.

UPDATE · This is the reason why good rehabs like to separate the men and the women. The very first thing that comes back after you've detoxed is your hormones. At BFC we weren't even allowed to talk to the men, which makes it even hotter. All I ever thought about was sneaking off with some dude and doing it behind the washing machine or meeting up in the middle of the night and hiding out in some shady corner while he fucked the shit out of me. The fantasy I had going on the airplane was being the only female teacher or, let's say, the only female guidance counselor at a school like the one in *Dead Poets Society*. I was a young-enough teacher so it wouldn't seem gross and all the boys would come to my office and ask me for "guidance." Oh who am I kidding? It's still that fantasy. Don't tell!

DECEMBER 2002 · NEW YORK CITY-AGE 23

DEAR DIARY,
So I asked Cindy to be my sponsor and she said yes

but she wanted me to be around every day because she didn't want me to relapse. So then she said she would give me a job for $10 an hour. So now she's my sponsor and my boss and I just love her so much. She has really helped me. I don't think I'd be able to do this without her. We also go out at night together which makes it easier, because we both order Shirley Temples. I have gained a lot of weight and don't have a crush on anyone and for the first time I really don't care. I actually feel happy.

UPDATE · Cindy ran a clothing line based out of a tiny studio on Christie Street. Now it's like a million-dollar enterprise. I like to think I played a small part in that! Cindy was exactly the person I needed in my life at that time. I was a lost little soul; she helped me find my way. I even got to go to Japan with her. She showed me that you don't have to be drunk to sing karaoke or dance like a retard or play charades at a bar when everyone else is telling the same drunken stories over and over. She helped me earn my silly wings. Today she is one of my best friends, although no longer my sponsor or my boss, which is for the best. One person can't be all those things. If there were a therapy term for that, I think it would be something like "Emotional Incest."

JULY 2003 · NEW YORK CITY-AGE 24

DEAR DIARY,
I moved out of my apartment. I had to get out of that crack den, too many bad memories. I am think-

ing about doing assistant styling, which could be good money. Heather said she needs someone. I think this sounds like a really good idea.

DEAR DIARY,

I love styling. I am trying to put a book together so I don't have to keep working under people. I met Justin Timberlake and stole his wife beater for Katie. I also made him call her. He was really nice, one of the better celebrities I've worked with. He was so nice to Kate when he called. I'm glad I had the balls to ask him to do that.

UPDATE · My sister, Katie, was very psyched that he called indeed. That was one of the better moments of being a stylist. I had made a lot of fashiony-type connections via Cindy, so I landed the styling gig pretty easily. A lot of it had to do with luck and having good connections. I realize that even when I complained about it, I never had to sit in a cubicle so I was just being whiny. (It could be a lot worse than meeting celebrities and going on trips for a living.) One of the big secrets about working in that industry is that you don't have to have brains or even great style to be a successful stylist. You don't need a diploma or a degree or even an expensive pair of shoes. What you need is upper-body strength to carry loads of garment bags up and down stairs, and you need to not bitch about doing it. You need to put in hours and time, and even if you don't know who Yves

Saint Laurent is, you will after the first week. It's about the easiest job around.

Oh yeah, another good moment was dancing around with Juliette Lewis. The worst celebrity I ever worked with was Pharell. He literally whispered, "What's my name, boo?" to the other assistant and then asked her what her sign was. He then got on the phone with a company in Brooklyn that made gold teeth and demanded they come into Manhattan and size him for caps. We tried to tell him that there were 2,894,239 places to get gold teeth on Delancey, but he wasn't having it. He came to the studio with five assistants, and they each ordered from a different restaurant. They ordered, like, oxtail soup from a place uptown that didn't even deliver and then made the photographer's intern go fetch it. I got so sick of styling because no one ever seemed to act like this behavior was fucked up. At one point another famous hip-hop dude we worked with had like four hookers from Queens come over to the shoot. Naomi Campbell wouldn't put on her own socks. Eva Mendes told us she had no idea how to act and hated it and it was funny that people paid her to do it. She said she was cashing in on the moment and then retiring.

I hated how everyone I worked with, even the cool photographers and stylists and people who are still my friends, would just kiss their asses so hard. Someone would suddenly demand a rocking horse covered in lullabies and no one batted an eye. After a while, working in this field started to make me die a little bit inside. I wanted to want to do it. I made great money and got fabulous gifts and clothes, went to fashion week and even had a seat there, but after a while it just wasn't worth it. I was ready to start working with blind people or something. Whatever the opposite of vanity was.

MARCH 2003 · NEW YORK CITY-AGE 25

DEAR DIARY,
I fucking hate styling. I swear, every time I do a job I say it's my last job and then I do another one. I guess it's the only thing I have right now. I actually regret not ever taking a business course when I was in college. I remember when my mom suggested that. Turns out she was right because now I have no skills and no fucking idea what I'm going to do with my life.

UPDATE · I loved going to Hampshire because I partied and made a lot of friends and learned a lot of stuff like don't use your credit card and "Beer before liquor, never get sicker; liquor before beer and you're in the clear," but majoring in creative writing only ever helped me to write a lot in my diary.

Being sober doesn't promise great jobs or flawless skin or husband and babies and a little house in Vermont. The only thing not drinking promises is that you won't get drunk. That and that I don't have to drink. I have a choice now. That doesn't make life easier. In fact, it makes it harder.

I quit styling after a friend hooked me up with a job at a hotel. It wasn't working with blind people, but it was something. And besides, I figured it would only be temporary until I found a "real" job. Two years later and I'm still at the hotel contemplating what that "real" job is.

AFTERWORD

✳

Even after 17 years of writing stuff down, I'm still insecure. I tried to think of a lot of ways to get around writing that sentence, and after erasing a million different versions I decided to get back to basics and just write a diary entry. Part of the reason we write in diaries is that we know we never have to show it to anyone. This relieves us of the pressure of having to please people. When I was growing up, I thought I had to please everyone: teachers, my parents, my friends, and pretty much anyone who "mattered." It was when I felt I had disappointed someone when I was most unhappy. If a boy didn't like me, surely it was because I wasn't attractive enough. When I fought with my friends it was because of something I had done wrong, even if I hadn't. I found I was always most comfortable in the role of the victim. In the back of my head there was always the fantasy of having my diary published. After I read *Anne Frank: The Diary of a Young Girl*, written by someone who actually was a victim, I envisioned a secret audience reading my diary as I wrote. The more I envisioned the audience, the more real the idea of one became. I would wish that one day I would be special, that I would be early and the rest of the world would be late. I dreamed that one day everyone would understand my pain (see Hampshire College 1997–2001). When I took my first poetry class the summer of 1994 I actually rewrote entries that came straight from my diary and just changed the line format. Whether or not they were good at the time didn't matter (they were amazing). What mattered was that I did it and it worked. At first I felt like I was tricking someone or cheating on a test. When the poetry teacher approached me, she praised me for the "voice" in my poems and how quickly I had adopted such style. It wasn't style to me; it was just everything true I had been feeling and never wanted to say. There was no catch to writing, and that's when I fell in love. Writing could be public or private. It could be done anywhere, and it could sound however I wanted it to. It would never be something I would need to please. I got addicted to writing because I wasn't trying to make anyone else happy and I didn't have to have a reason to do it or to love it—I just know that I did, and when someone else read it, it changed shape. What was once written in a locked-up book on a plain sheet of pink paper had turned into something I could use to communicate with. This is how a girl who was so insecure once upon a time turned into someone who would let the entire world read her diary today. I wrote more and more and more. I grew up. Somewhere along the line I got bitten by the truth bug. Once I started I couldn't stop. I don't know why this happened; maybe the chemical formula was, like, 3 ounces of punk music, a bushel of booze, and a peck of pot. Regardless, I told people everything about me, open-book style. I couldn't keep a secret for shit.

I had some great life lessons along my journey, and I'm a lot stronger than the girl they used to call Barfin Arfin back in 1991, although she has been known to show up from time to time, begging the world to feel bad for her. It's easy to slip into that whole "Woe is me" thing.

When I heard *Vice* was looking for a new writer for their "Dear Diary" column, I knew immediately it was for me. Since extremely low self-esteem is actually thinly disguised narcissism, every time I tried to write about anything but my own experiences it sounded fake. It felt good to finally surrender to my ego. At first I figured it might not be that interesting, "A 14-year-old girl feels self-conscious? Stop the presses!" My challenge was to turn the boring stuff into life-changing events, the embarrassing bits into humorous ones, and the pathetic moments into important learning experiences. As it turns out I didn't have to try very hard. What I realized was that the boring times were actually life changing. When I had "nothing to do" I found myself writing. The embarrassing stuff I went through, that was all comedic gold. Most important, though, I realized the moments I had deemed "pathetic" were really just regular old growing pains that everyone has. I realized I wasn't unique or "special," and my ego deflated. That was when the magic really happened.

My diary entries became not just my life story. They're every girl's life story. You're not me, but you're kind of me. You may not have had your ass kicked by your dad, learned how to weigh coke by a junkie named Skittles, or let a bi-curious ex-cheerleader on K eat you out in the bathtub, but you made a hundred mistakes and you survived. In fact, it's the mistakes that made you who you are today.

This book is about every girl who was totally left out but crushed out on the cutest boy in school anyway. It's about anyone who's ever looked up to someone they thought was cool and then realized that person is kind of a dick. It's about how amazingly shitty it is to be a teenage girl and how much you hate it when you're there and how much your heart swells when you look back on it as a grown-up. I hope everyone who reads it makes as many mistakes as I did. Just remember that mistakes are only worth it if they get written down in a diary. If you're lost at sea in your late 20s and you don't know what to do with your life, maybe you'll be able to convince someone to publish it.

PHOTO BY BILL STROBECK

ABOUT THE AUTHOR

Lesley Arfin was born in Long Island, NY. She graduated with a BA from Hampshire College in 2001. Besides writing the "Dear Diary" column in *Vice*, she has written a number other articles for them, including "The Vice Guide to Guilty Pleasure" and "The Vice Guide to Finding Yourself," both of which appeared in *The Vice Guide to Sex, Drugs, and Rock n Roll*, published by Warner Books. Her work has also appeared in *Jane*, *iD*, *Nylon*, *Paper*, and *Fashion Now 2*. Today she lives in New York City. She is 28 years old.